PREACHERS *of* RIGHTEOUSNESS

Yours in the Truth,

Steve Carney

II Peter 2:9

PREACHERS *of* RIGHTEOUSNESS

Those Who Walked with God

STEVE CARNEY

WinePress Publishing (PO Box 428, Enumclaw, WA 98022) functions only as book publisher. As such, the ultimate design, content, editorial accuracy, and views expressed or implied in this work are those of the author.

The author of this book has waived a portion of the publisher's recommended professional editing services. As such, any related errors found in this finished product are not the responsibility of the publisher.

Unless otherwise noted, all Scriptures are taken from the *Holy Bible, New International Version*®, *NIV*®. Copyright © 1973, 1978, 1984 by Biblica, Inc.™ Used by permission of Zondervan. All rights reserved worldwide. www.zondervan.com

ISBN 13: 978-1-4141-2354-7
ISBN 10: 1-4141-2354-X
Library of Congress Catalog Card Number: 2012906220

Dedicated to the Rev. Billy Graham,
a Preacher of Righteousness

CONTENTS

Brothers, think of what you were when you were called. Not many of you were wise by human standards; not many were influential; not many were of noble birth. But God chose the foolish things of the world to shame the wise; God chose the weak things of the world to shame the strong. He chose the lowly things of this world and the despised things—and the things that are not—to nullify the things that are, so that no one may boast before him.

—1 Corinthians 1:26-29

PREFACE

~⁂◯

THE SPIRIT SAID to Ezekiel, "I am sending you to them, and you must say to them: This is what the Lord God says. Whether they listen or refuse to listen …" (Ezekiel 2:4-5).

God desires the reader to remember the message more than the men who gave the message; the message that we can repent and get our lives in order because He is soon returning to earth to live with men.

What constitutes a preacher of righteousness? To be sure, those of us who've made Jesus the Lord of our lives have access to the Father through His blood. In essence, we, as believers in Christ, are all preachers of righteousness. We can all walk with God as Enoch walked. Still, those who were called preachers of righteousness in the Bible had some characteristics which set them apart. One purpose of this book is to reveal these attributes. As we shall see, perhaps their most distinctive attributes lie in their common purpose.

Why does God want us to remember His preachers of righteousness? It's not to worship these men, but to glorify God and honor these preachers as His servants. God wants us to remember their lives of obedience and the message they preached; the message that God is continually involved in the affairs of men. He will hold mankind accountable for his choices and deeds. He will forgive us of our sins if we believe and surrender to Christ. Because God is love, He administers justice and judgment to protect mankind from destroying himself and His universe. Judgment can only be avoided through repentance and faith in Jesus Christ. God wants mankind to fellowship with Him just as these preachers of righteousness did.

Interwoven throughout the book is the reoccurring theme of divine destiny. Each person born on the earth has a unique destiny for God's purposes, but not all find or fulfill their destiny. From Enoch to Finney, the preachers of righteousness mentioned in this book were men who knew their purpose and found their destiny. Sometimes one's lack of faith will prevent him from seeing God's purpose for his life. If through unbelief, one fails to see God' purposes, he will fall short of fulfilling his destiny. This book was penned to inspire the reader to find God's purpose for his life and live out his destiny. It was also written to inspire the reader to walk with God, just as the preachers of righteousness fellowshipped with Him.

Section one tells the story of a fictional preacher of righteousness. I believe this fictional story is a prophetic account of things to come in the church.

Section two gives accounts about preachers of righteousness who were mentioned in the Bible. It applies their lives and the truth they preached to today's generation. It's based on the Biblical accounts, but also contains some characteristics of a novel. As we research the scriptures, and the lives of other righteous men and women which have actually been recorded, it's not difficult to imagine their circumstances and what these men faced.

Needless to say, the means of communication was much less sophisticated in these ancient times. We have very limited accounts of what happened in these holy men's lives. For example, Noah lived so many years, it probably would have taken volumes of writing to recount all the episodes; how God dealt with the people of Noah's generation, the Holy Spirit's pleading with the people through Noah; the people's reaction; the persecution of Noah and his family. Indeed, just as modern day preachers of righteousness, I feel it safe to say these ancient preachers of righteousness endured much hardship and opposition. I wanted to understand their unique calling and relationship with God.

Section three summarizes the revivals of Charles G. Finney taken from his original memoirs. Unlike the Biblical preachers of righteousness, Finney recorded many of his experiences in a book of memoirs. For an extensive writing of Finney's life, I recommend *The Original Memoirs of Charles G. Finney*, with Garth M. Rosell and Richard A. G. Dupuis, editors. Unlike the people of Noah's generation who refused to repent, Finney had wonderful results with many conversions to Jesus Christ, as he preached. At the same time, the powers of darkness stirred up opposition wherever he went, much like the Apostle Paul.

Trusting the Holy Spirit's guidance, I gathered divine truths from Finney's memoirs. I mention only those spiritual principals which contribute to the themes prevalent in *Preachers of Righteousness* as it applies to our generation; the themes of judgment, sincere repentance, salvation through Jesus Christ, persecution, pure motives, and an intimate walk with God.

Some of you may wonder why Jesus wasn't included in *Preachers of Righteousness*. Jesus is not simply a preacher of righteousness. The Messiah *is* righteousness and truth. Indeed, He is God's Son, the Savior of the world, set apart from God's creation. For this reason, I felt it would be somewhat irreverent to include Jesus with men. To write about Jesus, the Son of God, one needs to devote a whole separate book. Like the other preachers of righteousness, Jesus preached repentance. The Son of God warned of judgments to come. He specifically mentioned the judgment of Jerusalem; how the city would be leveled to the ground because the city didn't recognize the time of His visitation. As He drew near and saw Jerusalem, He wept over it (Luke 19:41-44).

Each preacher of righteousness was sent to prepare the people for a major purpose and event on God's timetable. Enoch was sent to turn men from their wicked ways so they wouldn't be destroyed. He prophesied of Christ's return with ten thousand of his saints to judge the ungodly. Noah also preached repentance and warned of the great flood. Elijah was sent to bring Israel out of idolatry. John the Baptist preached repentance, preparing the way for the Messiah. God anointed Charles Finney to expose deception and false doctrines in the Church. Finney also warned of judgment and the way to escape judgment through Jesus Christ. God used Finney to usher in a refreshing revival for the United

States of America, a revival which brought in a great harvest of souls shortly before judgment fell upon the land in the form of the Civil War.

The preachers of righteousness were some unique individuals. What was each one's purpose, and what set him apart? What did each have in common? What were their possible thoughts? How did they obtain such favor with God? How did they cope with the persecutions?

Let me introduce you to the preachers of righteousness. They have much to teach us. Let's humble ourselves and learn from them. If you join them, you'll enter into God's very presence. Come and dine at His table. Come walk with Him in the garden. He will lead you to safety, just as He did the preachers of righteousness. You will be spared from the terrible judgments which are yet to come.

Part I

HE WILL SHOW YOU
THINGS TO COME

Chapter 1

FEAR GOD AND GIVE HIM GLORY

THE PREACHER STEPPED up to the pulpit as the congregation waited with anticipation and deafening silence. He opened the ancient scriptures and read from the book of Acts:

> Repent, then, and turn to God, so that your sins may be wiped out, that times of refreshing may come from the Lord, and that he may send the Christ, who has been appointed for you—even Jesus.
> —Acts 3:19-20

In divine inspiration resembling John the Baptist, Benjamin continued, "Let the unclean be made clean. Let the crooked be made straight. All flesh will see the glory of the Lord. God's truth shall fill the earth as the waters cover the sea (Isaiah 11:9, Habakkuk 2:14). Turn from lawlessness! Obey God's commandments. Obey His Holy Spirit and live! Fear God and give glory to Him; for the hour of his judgment is come" (Revelation 14:7). He paused and waited without a word. As he waited, the Lord's presence began to fill the place as a soft breeze or a fine mist.

He walked off the platform and a silence filled the congregation as the people waited with anticipation. Although Benjamin withdrew from the platform and joined the congregation, nobody left the building.

Indeed, no one dared to move. God's presence grew stronger each minute, as a crescendo in a classic symphony. There was an awareness of God's holiness and purity. A great light shined in the conscience of every soul, exposing dark secrets. Blind eyes were opened to see; to see wrong motives; to see fearful thoughts of unbelief; to see malice. Worldly minds were stripped, revealing impure thoughts. The deaf ears were opened to hear the gospel of Jesus Christ. People everywhere began to weep in repentance. Tears begin to flow, as some cried softly. The relative silence was broken only by the occasional moans and wailing of repentant souls. There was no doubt in anyone's mind that God, not man, was running this show. Some became unsettled and abruptly left the meeting refusing to deal with things they could not see nor understand. Rather than surrender to Jesus Christ, they fled from His convicting presence, refusing to deal with their sins. As if on cue, others began to run to the altar. Some fell on their knees weeping in the Lord's presence. Some cried so hard they shook with convulsions.

Among them was a man named Frank. Frank was in an accident a few months ago. He had been helping his brother cut down a dead pine tree in his yard. He was holding the chain saw in his right hand while trying to hold a limb steady with the other. The chain saw slipped cutting off his left hand at the wrist. His brother tried to stop the bleeding. He rushed Frank to the emergency room. As Frank got out of the car he began to pass out. The medics carried him inside. Frank's brother also brought Frank's hand, hoping the surgeon could graft it back on his arm, but to no avail. The doctors sewed up his wrist and stopped the bleeding, but Frank's hand was lost. It still seemed like a terrible nightmare for Frank. He had lost a great deal of blood. He was just thankful to still be alive.

But Frank wasn't even thinking about his hand right now. Until now, Frank was never fully convinced the Bible was totally true. He believed Jesus was a good man who taught the truth of how we should live, but was somewhat skeptical concerning the miracles and couldn't buy into the claims Christ was born of a virgin or that He arose from the dead. But today upset his theology. For the first time in his life, he sensed God's awesome presence. It made the hair on the back of his neck stand up. Although he rushed to the altar with the fear of God, he also felt God's love. He saw for the first time the sacrifice Jesus had made for him. Frank wanted to trust Him and to know Him. He had never witnessed such love or power.

"God, please forgive me and help me to change," Frank mumbled to himself. As he prayed this prayer his body relaxed. All the stress and tension vanished. Frank knew in his heart that he was forgiven. *This is the most peaceful I've felt since I was a child*, Frank thought.

Soon the congregation began to worship spontaneously in the Spirit. Their voices rose in perfect harmony like an angelic choir. All eyes were closed, as hearts were focused on the King of kings. Many were so focused on Christ; they were carried away into a heavenly state of mind, unaware of those standing next to them. As the worship continued, the gentle breeze became a mighty wind.

"Holy is the Lord!" shouted someone in the crowd. God was revealing Himself in power. Some in the congregation shook as though a thousand volts of electricity flowed through their bodies.

Frank felt warmth in his belly. Then it went up to his lungs. Soon he was shaking with the Holy Spirit's power. He felt warmth on the stub of his wrist where his hand was missing. With eyes closed and tears in his eyes Frank continued to worship the Lord.

Frank opened his eyes and was amazed at what he saw. Right before his eyes Frank had a perfectly developed hand where it once was but a stub. It seemed like a dream, a wonderful dream! In his excitement Frank bolted onto the platform and with tears of joy, related to the congregation what great things God had done for him.

Upon hearing Frank's testimony, the congregation roared with excitement. Some began to literally scream. Many who were sick received healing. Others fell under the Holy Spirit's power experiencing a rest which was not of this world. People began shouting praises to God. The worship team broke out in song and people began to dance before the Lord with great joy and enthusiasm. This lasted for about thirty minutes. The worship then changed to quiet gentle songs and gradually ceased.

The mighty wind of the Spirit, the Conductor of this marvelous worship, moved into a diminuendo and a calm peace filled the air; the cadence of a marvelous composition ending in a tranquil silence. There was a sense of victory, completeness, and wholeness. No one wanted to leave God's presence.

This was, by far, the largest church Benjamin had ever spoken at. Though he preached at small churches for several years, nothing of this magnitude had ever occurred. The fact that God used him in such a marvelous way made him feel deeply humble and grateful.

At this point, Benjamin slipped out of the building, unnoticed by the people. God was finished with him here. God was doing the work and Benjamin had to decrease so God could increase. He opened the door to his modest car and started the engine. As clouds began to gather and the wind began to blow, Benjamin pulled out of the church parking lot. He had the deep satisfaction of a mission completed. He'd spend some time alone with God. It was time to rest and await further instructions as he prepared for the next meeting. As he drove out of town, he remembered how God had prepared him for this day.

The Lord Calls Benjamin

Benjamin grew up as an only child in the wilderness of Alaska. His father was a forest ranger at Kobuk Valley National Park. They lived in the small town of Kiana. His mother was from an orthodox Jewish family prior to receiving Jesus as the Messiah. Consequently, Benjamin had practiced many traditional feasts and customs of the orthodox Jews. His mother taught him the Torah, the Psalms, the prophets, the feasts, and the New Testament from an early age. She often emphasized how all in the Bible pointed to Jesus, the Messiah. Through the years Benjamin had deep worship experiences while observing these feasts. He memorized many scriptures as a child.

As a toddler and child, he attended Sunday school and Vacation Bible School. A somewhat introverted child, he was always aware of God's presence. His parents were much disciplined with their faith. Some in their tiny church even warned them of being too religious and legalistic. But Benjamin's wise mother knew the gravity of obedience to God's Word and the Holy Spirit. Indeed, it made the difference between blessing and cursing, life and death.

His mom often told Benjamin the story of how Jesus appeared to her in a dream proclaiming, "You will conceive a son and call his name

Benjamin. He will be one of many who will prepare my Bride, for I am coming soon. Guard him from every unclean thing of the world. He is to live a holy life separated unto me. He will learn to hear my voice and will learn obedience through his sufferings." At age twelve, Benjamin received a baptism in the Holy Spirit's power while celebrating the feast of Pentecost.

Benjamin and his parents lived in a modest home resembling a log cabin in the Alaskan wilderness. They didn't have cable vision or satellite television. His father only allowed a few simple video games such as Pac Man. They did own a PC and DVD player, but his parents restricted his time on them. Occasionally, Benjamin was able to watch some clean family movies together with his mom and dad. Each family member also had a cell phone in case of emergency in this sparsely populated area of rough country. There weren't many children in Benjamin's small school; only a few boys near his age. Besides his school studies and chores, Benjamin loved to read. He used his imagination to invent fun games. He loved to go sledding and skiing in the snow.

During the summer months, he spent most of his time outdoors. He loved the Alaskan wilderness. Sometimes, he'd go with his dad to the national park. His dad trained him well in wilderness survival. As he grew older, Benjamin spent much of his time in the summer hunting, fishing, and enjoying the wilds. Much of his time was spent alone. Benjamin carried his Bible on his ventures into the wilderness and spent hours studying God's Word.

It was during these times Benjamin learned to hear God's voice. On his journeys through the wilderness, God visited him. Joy, peace, and love filled him as he worshiped God in the Alaskan backwoods. Benjamin's experiences on these journeys were more than pleasant; they were exhilarating.

He always looked forward to observing the birds and small animals. The sound of wildlife was soothing, peaceful, comforting; almost like medicine to his mind, body, and emotions. After a stressful day with his studies, Benjamin liked to venture into the wilderness. The birds sang their melodies as if joyfully singing to the Lord. *How marvelous is God's creation*, Benjamin thought with delight over and over, as he was overcome with praise and worship.

At age eighteen, Benjamin's father helped him get a job as a ranger and he worked in an Alaskan wild refuge park. Benjamin thought, *How blessed to have a job I love. How many people are able to delight in getting up each morning and going into work?* During his times in the wilds, Benjamin learned to discern the Holy Spirit's still small voice. He received much revelation and learned about his purpose and calling.

Benjamin still remembers how on a clear summer night when at age thirty years old, God called him out of the Alaskan wilderness to preach.

"Follow me and I will make you a fisher of men. Step out of the boat and you will walk on the water. You have finished your preparation. Now is the time for you to enter into your calling. You must leave your home in Kiana," the Holy Spirit whispered into Benjamin's conscience.

Benjamin inquired, *Lord, where shall I go?*

"Leave your father and mother, and I will show you where to go. As I revealed, you will prepare the way for my soon return. I'm coming for a spotless bride, a small remnant who has kept their garments white from the stains of the world. I have called you among others to help purify her and prepare the way. I will give you the words you should speak," came the reply.

Benjamin wasn't anxious to leave his peaceful surroundings; the comforts; the good home cooked meals; his father and mother's love. After all, he was able to enjoy God's presence in the wilderness. He felt uncomfortable around people, especially crowds. Benjamin thought to himself, *I'd rather stay here in God's presence.* The still small voice spoke again, "My presence will be with you wherever you go."

This wasn't really what Benjamin wanted to hear. To give up this beautiful Alaskan wilderness; to leave the love and security of his home was a hard pill to swallow. He felt very content where he was. It suited him just fine if he lived the rest of his life like his father in the national park reserve. As Benjamin contemplated the cost, he put off answering God's call and continued his daily routines.

But as time went on Benjamin began to sense a driving force of motivation. God's Word was like a fire in his bones; burning like red hot coals with such zeal he could hardly contain it (Jeremiah 20:9). A few months later, the Holy Spirit moved upon Benjamin once again. One morning during his daily devotions the scriptures leaped off the page as if Jesus was speaking directly to him. "Benjamin, do you love me?" The question pierced through his innermost being.

"There is no one I'd rather fellowship with than with you, Lord," Benjamin responded. Having read the entire Bible several times, Benjamin knew what was coming next.

"Then feed my sheep", the tender voice replied (John 21:15-19).

Benjamin thought of the sacrifice Jesus had made for him; how Jesus was accused falsely, ridiculed and beaten; how He hung on a cross and cried out with a loud voice, "It is finished!" Jesus paid the ultimate price so Benjamin's sins could be forgiven. After all Jesus had done for him, how could he refuse his dearest friend? God's love would sustain him through any trial or circumstance. Jesus had given His all, how could Benjamin do any less? Besides, he was acquainted with God well enough to know that he couldn't be truly content outside of His will.

He didn't wait for Jesus to ask him again. With sincerity and willingness of heart Benjamin cried out, "Here I am Lord, send me" (Isaiah 6:8). He had been so concerned about leaving the security of his home; the comfort and beauty of his surroundings in the Alaskan wilderness; he had never stopped to think about Jesus' words in the gospels. Jesus had declared those who left all for Him would receive a hundred times more in this life. And even better, they'd inherit eternal life (Matthew 19:29-30). Never in his dreams had Benjamin imagined all the wonderful things in store for him along with great persecutions.

As raindrops began to splatter on the windshield, Benjamin was brought back to the present day reality. Now only a year later, God had opened many doors for him before church congregations. The people recognized the anointing; that he had been with Jesus. God had opened a door no man could shut (Revelation 3:8). Benjamin's powerful preaching caused people to either love or hate him. There was no indifference toward him. He was treated as royalty by some and as the earth's scum by others. There were those who wanted to bless Benjamin; those who wanted him to run for political office, and those who denounced him as a hatemonger; those who threatened his very life.

However, no one could deny the signs and wonders which followed Benjamin's preaching. His message brought people to the valley of decision. His was a message of change; a message of repentance. However, it wasn't Benjamin's message, but God's message. Benjamin was one of God's spokespersons for his generation. He was sent for a specific mission; to prepare the way of the Lord.

He felt amazed and in awe by God's mighty demonstration of power, especially in the worship service that night. *Our God is an awesome God,* he whispered to himself. As Benjamin pondered what had just transpired, the reverential fear of God came upon him. The lightning flashed and the thunder roared as if to manifest God's awesome power. Benjamin shuddered as he drove on into the night.

Korah's Rebellion

One month later Benjamin found himself speaking at a small church called Bible Fellowship Church, a stark contrast to the mega church of his previous campaign. Although Benjamin was never much for titles, the pastor introduced him as God's prophet. He just spoke what God told him to speak and did what God told him to do. He was more concerned about the harvest of souls; the earth's precious fruit. Even so, Benjamin was deeply humbled even to the point of tears when God performed signs and wonders during the meetings.

When admirers lavished praise upon him, Benjamin sometimes replied, "I've sinned just as everyone else. I have past failures and human weaknesses. I'm no better than anyone in the congregation. What I am, I am by the grace of God."

Benjamin never forgot it was only Christ's sacrifice that saved him from death, hell, destruction and eternal damnation.

Why have you chosen me through which to demonstrate such mighty works? Benjamin once asked.

"Because I can trust you," answered the Lord.

Benjamin still hadn't received a word from the Lord, so he waited on the Lord for his sermon topic. As usual he trusted God to give him divine utterance—the message for this particular congregation. He felt a cloud of skepticism and unbelief as he stood behind the pulpit, so he asked the worship leader to lead the congregation in one more song. As the choir continued in worship Benjamin received these words over and over in his spirit: *Korah's rebellion; Korah's rebellion.* As the worship had ended he managed to forge ahead. He began speaking on God's authority and how God appointed men to rule and subdue the earth. Next, he showed from the scriptures how God appointed certain men for specific projects and seasons. God gave them authority and power to complete the task.

"It's dangerous to rebel against righteous leaders whom God has appointed over us in authority," he solemnly warned. He read examples from the Bible of what happened to those who rebelled against God's appointed authorities.

"Saul continually persecuted David and even tried to kill him. He betrayed him and did evil against David. And yet, David refused to take revenge or speak evil of King Saul, even though he knew he had been anointed to replace Saul as king of Israel," explained Benjamin (1 Samuel 26:9-11).

He told the story of Korah's rebellion against Moses as recorded in Numbers chapter 16:

"Because Moses was the meekest man upon the earth, some among the Hebrews had problems accepting his authority and leadership. They refused to recognize the fact that God had appointed Moses to lead the people of Israel," asserted Benjamin.

"Perhaps they had mistaken meekness as being weak. Weakness comes with being fearful. Meekness involves love, humility and self-control. Weakness entails self-ambition and the fear of man. Meekness is submitting to one another, serving one another, preferring others as better than yourselves (Philippians 2:3). Meekness is having restrained power. A perfect example of meekness is Jesus in the garden of Gethsemane the night of His betrayal. He could have called legions of angels to defend Him, but chose to humble Himself and allow the soldiers to arrest Him" (Matthew 26:53).

As Benjamin continued, he noticed the anointing increasing, "Perhaps Moses wasn't the deliverer the Israelites had imagined. His meekness was probably mistaken for weak leadership. In addition, his stuttering made him appear less than a formidable hero. They may have noticed some character flaws in Moses. Possibly Moses lacked the aggressiveness or assertiveness found in most successful leaders. Since he was meek, he wasn't the forceful commander many Hebrews had expected. He lacked the 'take charge' type of attitude that attracts many followers.

Maybe Moses didn't have a charming personality. Being human, Moses likely made an occasional mistake in judgment, such as striking the rock instead of speaking to it, as God had instructed" (Numbers 20:7-12).

Benjamin continued the story, "For whatever reason, Korah, along with 250 other leaders who had been appointed as members of the council rebelled against Moses and Aaron. These men were intelligent respected leaders with talent and high character. Their proven record of leadership, experience, and wisdom led to their being appointed on the council. The council was no doubt a distinguished place of leadership among the Hebrews, which now numbered over a million (Numbers 16:2). However, these men still had one character flaw—pride."

Benjamin paused just long enough to catch his breath, "They argued with Moses, 'The whole community is holy. Why do you set yourself up above the rest of us?' God had placed His Spirit of wisdom and council upon these leaders. They had been used by God in marvelous ways. But in their pride, they failed to believe that God, and not men, had appointed Moses and Aaron. When Moses heard these rebellious words he fell with his face to the ground. He knew these men were inviting calamity upon themselves and their families. Our God is a consuming fire" (Hebrews 12:29).

The congregation was now fully attentive as Benjamin continued, "Then Moses said to Korah and all his followers: 'In the morning the Lord will show who belongs to him and who is holy, and he will have that person come near him. The man he chooses; he will cause to come near him. You, Korah, and all your followers are to do this: Take censers and tomorrow put fire and incense in them before the Lord. The man the Lord chooses will be the one who is holy. You Levites have gone too far'" (Numbers 16:5-7)!

Benjamin went on to explain, "Moses saw that Korah and his followers had overstepped their authority. They had coveted Moses' position of authority, trying to operate in the office of priesthood for which they were not called. They wanted control, and were determined to do things their way instead of following God's instructions given through Moses."

The congregation of Bible Fellowship Church listened as Benjamin told the story, "Moses also said to Korah, 'Now listen, you Levites! Isn't it enough for you that the God of Israel has separated you from the rest of the Israelite community and brought you near himself to do the work at the Lord's tabernacle and to stand before the community and minister to them? He has brought you and all your fellow Levites near himself, but now you are trying to get the priesthood too. It is against the Lord that you and all your followers have banded together'" (Numbers 16:8-11).

Benjamin stressed this important truth, "Notice Korah and his followers weren't rebelling just against Moses, but against the Lord as well. Then Moses summoned Dathan and Abiram, the sons of Eliab. But they said, 'We will not come! Isn't it enough that you have brought us up out of a land flowing with milk and honey to kill us in the desert? And now you also want to lord it over us? Moreover, you haven't brought us into a land flowing with milk and honey or given us an inheritance of fields and vineyards. Will you gouge out the eyes of these men? No, we will not come!' This made Moses very angry. Then Moses instructed Korah and his followers to appear before the Lord the next day. They met with Moses, Aaron, and the Lord. The entire assembly of Israel was present to witness the power struggle."

By now God's manifested presence filled the congregation as Benjamin spoke under the anointing. Unknowingly to Benjamin, the little church had been going through difficult times. Some in the church were stirring up strife and planting seeds of rebellion against the pastor. As a result, tithes were down and the small congregation was struggling to pay its bills. Some had even left the church. The pastor hadn't mentioned this to Benjamin, but the church congregation was well aware of the power struggle going on between the pastor and certain members in the congregation. Some leaders in the church envied the pastor. Convinced they could do a better job, they also wanted the prestige and honor which they believed came with the pastor's office. The pastor had graciously volunteered to take a cut in pay.

God's Swift Justice

The people were on the edge of their seats as Benjamin continued, "The Lord said to Moses and Aaron, 'Separate from this assembly so I can put an end to them at once.' God was about to destroy the whole assembly of Israelites. But Moses interceded for them and cried out, 'O God, God of the spirits of all mankind, will you be angry with the entire assembly when only one man sins?'"

Benjamin paused briefly to allow the audience to reflect. Then he proceeded with the climax of the story, "So God told Moses and Aaron to separate themselves from the tents of Korah, Dathan and Abiram. Then Moses said, 'This is how you will know that the Lord has sent me to do all these things and that it was not my idea: If these men die a natural death and experience only what usually happens to men, then the Lord has not sent me. But if the Lord brings about something totally new, and the earth opens its mouth and swallows them, with everything that belongs to them, and they go down alive into the grave, then you will know that these men have treated the Lord with contempt.'"

Benjamin's voice resounded with authority as he spoke under the Holy Spirit's anointing, "As soon as he finished saying all this, the ground under them split apart and the earth opened its mouth and swallowed them, with their households and all Korah's men and all their possessions. They went down alive into the grave, with everything they owned; the earth closed over them, and they perished and were gone from the community. At their cries, all the Israelites around them fled, shouting, 'The earth is going to swallow us too!' And fire came out from the LORD and consumed the 250 men who were offering the incense."

Some of the church deacons in the congregation who were part of the power struggle began to tremble in their seats as God's awesome presence descended on the congregation. Benjamin gazed at the congregation with piercing eyes and declared, "Separate yourselves from the rebellion that you may be spared in the Day of Judgment." Many in the congregation began to softly weep tears of repentance and grief for having participated in the strife and discord within the church against their pastor.

As Benjamin continued, a main instigator of the church's rebellion stood and interrupted the flow of God's Spirit, "I know what you're doing and whom you're speaking about. You're no prophet of God! The pastor has put you up to this. You're a fake! You're of the devil and you deceive by the devil's power!" The man's face became flushed with anger. Suddenly, within a matter of seconds, he grabbed his chest and fell down dead. The fear of God swept through the congregation, as some began to panic. Someone came to administer first aid, but to no avail. Some in the congregation fled in fear. Someone with a cell phone dialed 911.

Benjamin was stunned, as he observed the situation. He felt sorrow over the man's fate. There was a foreboding finality to his death. He had blasphemed the Holy Spirit. Judgment had come and there was nothing the paramedics or anyone else could do about it. God had given the man plenty of time to repent, but his heart had become hardened. *If only he had humbled himself,* Benjamin thought.

> And so I tell you, every sin and blasphemy will be forgiven men, but the blasphemy against the Spirit will not be forgiven. Anyone who speaks a word against the Son of Man will be forgiven, but anyone who speaks against the Holy Spirit will not be forgiven, either in this age or in the age to come.
> —Matthew 12:31-32

Soon, the ambulance arrived. After an unsuccessful attempt to revive the man, they covered his body and carried him away. A newspaper reporter, somehow having heard of the incident, had arrived and began asking questions. Some who witnessed the tragedy recounted the scene.

"Where is this Benjamin?" the reporter quizzed. They began to look around trying to spot the man of God, but he was nowhere to be found. The next day, an article appeared in the small town newspaper describing the eerie event. The article later was picked up by the associated press and carried throughout the nation.

Benjamin found out later that this man had continually stirred up strife and opposed everything the pastor attempted. He was always critical and complaining about people in Bible Fellowship Church. Many in the church were apprehensive around this man. Some even feared him.

After this phenomenon occurred, some decided to leave the church, fearful that other such supernatural manifestations would occur. Most of those stirring up strife repented and began to submit to the pastor's leadership. The fires of revival spread from this small church. Some who had previously left the church because of the strife, returned when they heard of the revival. As news of the revival spread, many in the area came to Bible Fellowship Church, some just out of curiosity. Some drove many miles from other towns to participate in this great revival. The pastor preached with renewed faith and boldness. Many were converted and committed their lives to Christ. As church attendance increased, so did the tithes. The church was able to get out of debt. Benjamin was very please upon hearing the good news.

After the press carried the story about the strange phenomenon at Bible Fellowship Church, Benjamin's ministry became internationally known. Everywhere Benjamin went, he drew the crowds. As Benjamin continued traveling and preaching, other such occurrences followed. Supernatural signs and wonders followed his preaching. People came to the meetings with great faith and expectation. Many repented and surrendered their lives to God, receiving Jesus the Messiah as Lord and Savior. Many were healed and delivered, while supernatural manifestations occurred. Demons were cast out. Everywhere Benjamin went, God's presence manifested in a tangible way.

At the same time, awful judgment came upon some who actively opposed the revival meetings and blasphemed God. This began to stir up a great controversy within the Church. Some accused Benjamin of being harsh and mean spirited. He was labeled among some in the church as being a negative preacher. Others questioned his authority. They accused Benjamin of practicing witchcraft.

"God would never be involved in something such as this. It isn't God, but Satan doing these awful things. Benjamin gets his power from the devil," they reasoned.

Others defended Benjamin, "How could such healings, salvations, and miracles occur in this man's ministry if he is getting his power from the devil? I've felt God's love flow through this man. Many have committed their lives to the Lord Jesus Christ through his ministry."

As news spread concerning the supernatural manifestations in Benjamin's meetings, he couldn't be seen in public without people flocking over with curiosity or desperate need. At the same time, he was also receiving death threats from those who vehemently opposed the truth. With the persecution and lack of privacy, Benjamin thought about the similarities between his ministry and Christ's public ministry. He could now truly identify with Christ. He remembered the words Jesus told His disciples:

> When you are persecuted in one place, flee to another. I tell you the truth, you will not finish going through the cities of Israel before the Son of Man comes. A student is not above his teacher, nor a servant above his master. It is enough for the student to be like his teacher, and the servant like his master. If the head of the house has been called Beelzebub, how much more the members of his household! So do not be afraid of them. There is nothing concealed that will not be disclosed, or hidden that will not be made known. What I tell you in the dark, speak in the daylight; what is whispered in your ear, proclaim from the roofs. Do not be afraid of those who kill the body but cannot kill the soul. Rather be afraid of the One who can destroy both soul and body in hell.
>
> —Matthew 10:23-28

Benjamin often ministered to people to the point of exhaustion. He arose early before the crack of dawn to spend time in prayer. He sometimes looked for a place to be alone; to find time to escape the tremendous pressure of the ministry's fame and controversy. He'd find a place to get alone with God and be strengthened (Is. 40:31).

Had he truly counted the cost? He never imagined the intense spiritual warfare which he had recently encountered. He sometimes longed to return to his secure childhood home in Alaska; far away from the pressures of fame and persecution; breathing in the fresh arctic air with only the sound of birds, and the occasional howling of a wolf. But Benjamin knew in his heart those days were gone. He would not turn back. He would fight the good fight of faith. God's grace is sufficient. For the sake of the people, he would go forward and finish the race set before him.

The Elijah Generation

I believe the story of Benjamin is a revelation of things to come. God is in the process of anointing men and women in the spirit of Elijah to prepare the Church for her coming King. God is training preachers of righteousness like Enoch, Noah, Elijah, John the Baptist, and Charles Finney to warn men everywhere to repent and turn back to God. I believe the world is entering into the threshold of a new season similar to the times of these great men, climaxing in the return of Christ.

Consequently, it's relevant to examine their lives. Why did God choose these particular men to preach righteousness and warn of judgments to come? What set these men apart from the rest of the world? Why did many of their generation refuse to hear them? As we examine their lives, we'll see there were several similarities these men had in common.

There will be a holy remnant raised up within the Church before the Son of Man returns. Not only will we see great healings, salvations, and miracles take place through this holy remnant, but we will also see judgments as the world has never seen in this period of grace. Why such judgments? The period of grace is coming to an end. Soon Christ will come to separate the sheep from the goats, the wheat from the tares. His patience with man will come to an end and He will judge swiftly with a two edged sword. God is appointing judgments upon men which haven't been known since before the days of Christ. At the same time, we will see great miracles not seen since the days of the early Apostles. All of these things must take place, leading to the great tribulation period. The climax will be salvation for all virgins whose lamps are full of oil and the destruction of the wicked (Mat. 25:1-13). Are you ready?

Part II

Ancient Preachers
of
Righteousness

Chapter 2

ONE WHO WALKED WITH GOD

COME WITH ME to a time and place thousands of years ago; before there were modern technological advances; before the modern generation's hurried lifestyle; a time when servants, crops, and livestock was man's currency; camels, horses, donkeys, and walking by foot was the means of transportation. In those ancient days of physical hardship, people didn't spend their time looking for entertainment. Unless one had wealth and many servants, men and women spent all day just to provide food and clothing.

Much like today, people everywhere began to forget God. They became busy, struggling to provide food and clothing. They began to worship idols, relying on their idols for food, a bountiful harvest, and good luck. Soon they drifted into evil. God saw the evil and was grieved. If this evil were left unabated, Man would surely destroy himself. It was time for God to intervene and step into the affairs of Man. Since God is a merciful god, He won't pronounce judgment without warning. When God sent judgment upon the earth, there were always men and women with whom God confided. In the next few chapters, we will focus on men who walked with God. The Bible refers to these men as preachers of righteousness.

With the Holy Spirit's help, we will attempt to get into the mind and daily routines of these men. What was each one's purpose, and what set him apart? What did each have in common? How did they obtain such favor with God? How did they cope with the persecutions? What made these men so unique?

These preachers of righteousness were special because they walked with God. They were acquainted with the Creator of the universe. God had manifested Himself to them. He revealed Himself; His thoughts; His plans. God considered these preachers of righteousness His friends. He fellowshipped with them. These were ordinary men, made extraordinary by their creator.

God reveals His plans to those who respect Him, those whom He can trust. God sends men to warn of coming judgments. These were holy men skilled in righteousness, able to discern good and evil. Like sharp threshing instruments, they were sent to reveal the intent of men's hearts, to divide the wheat from the tares. Their words were like a shaft of light piercing the darkness around them.

Not only did they warn of judgment, but they also declared good news. God doesn't want mankind to destroy one another. He has provided a way out of judgment if men will repent and, in faith turn to Him. God will one day come to bring salvation and restore all things for those who respect Him and believe in Him. These prophets learned to listen to the Lord's voice and obey in faith. One day, they will rule with the Messiah from Jerusalem.

There are many such preachers of righteousness mentioned in the Bible. In the next four chapters, we will focus on four men who walked with God.

Enoch

Enoch was a preacher of righteousness. He lived a few hundred years before his great-grandson, Noah.

> When Enoch had lived 65 years, he became the father of Methuselah. And after he became the father of Methuselah, Enoch walked with God 300 years and had other sons and daughters. Altogether, Enoch lived 365 years. Enoch walked with God; then he was no more, because God took him away.
>
> —Genesis 5:21-24

There is little recorded in the Canon Bible concerning Enoch. However, we do have some scriptures as a reference to draw from. In addition, we can be relatively sure of some aspects of his life based on other preachers of righteousness whose lives are recorded in more detail. According to Moses' account in Genesis, Enoch walked with God for 300 years after Methuselah's birth. It was probably near the time of Methuselah's birth that God began to speak to Enoch.

The Hebrew translation of Methuselah's name is, "When he dies, it shall be sent." I believe God revealed to Enoch He was about to destroy the earth. It's probable he named his son Methuselah after this crucial revelation. Enoch may not have known all the details about the flood or how to escape it, as God later revealed to Noah. Nevertheless, God expressed to Enoch His displeasure over the sons of Man. Enoch had a vision of the Holy One and His angels who revealed to him things to come (Jude 1:14-15).

Methuselah, Enoch's son, lived longer than any other man on earth; 969 years. He was the son of Enoch and the grandfather of Noah. He lived five years after his son Lamech passed away. The flood came almost immediately after Methuselah's death. He was the last living being of his generation. Perhaps there were more honorable men and women living in Methuselah's generation than Noah's. God was waiting for Methuselah's generation to die out before the great flood came.

Could it be possible God is waiting for the World War II generation, also known as the greatest generation, to completely die out before he releases severe judgments on the present evils of this world; judgments never before known to mankind? I believe Rev. Billy Graham is a modern day preacher of righteousness. At the time of this writing he is in his early nineties. Could it be Rev. Graham's life span is the measuring rod for the time we have left before severe judgments are released on this present generation?

It's likely Noah heard from his grandfather, Methuselah, how Enoch had fellowshipped with God. According to the Bible, God took him away from the earth about 69 years before Noah was born. I believe Enoch told Methuselah and Lamech stories of God, just as many parents and grandparents do today. Enoch taught his sons and daughters to reverence God.

Enoch taught them about God's ways and how to hear His voice. Most likely Methuselah and Lamech listened to Enoch's words from God and they passed it on to Noah, Lamech's son, long after Enoch left the earth for a better place. I believe Noah and his offspring had access to Enoch's account of his walk with the Lord. Enoch's other descendants were too busy with the world's cares. They loved the things of the world more than God. They didn't have time to sit and listen to Enoch's tales about God. Consequently, their children perished in the flood. Only Noah and his family survived.

It's not difficult to imagine how Enoch may have been persecuted. It's highly plausible Enoch was treated with the same contempt and disrespect suffered by believers of the 21st century who take a stand for truth, justice, and righteousness. "What has been will be again, what has been done will be done again; there is nothing new under the sun." (Ecclesiastes 1:9)

The people of Enoch's generation may have considered him a bit strange. He was always talking as if he knew God. They didn't believe God talked to Enoch. Indeed, they had their doubts about whether this God truly did exist. If God existed, why had He not appeared to them? Besides, Enoch was preachy and made them feel uncomfortable. When he spoke of his visions of hell and eternal punishment for the wicked, they became fearful. They weren't willing to listen to such tales of doom and gloom.

Enoch stood out from the rest of mankind in character and integrity. His purity and good works convicted this generation of their sins. When they heard Enoch teach of God's truth and righteousness, their faults and shortcomings convicted them. They liked things the way they were and didn't want to change. They went out of the way to be conveniently absent when Enoch spoke about God's ways.

The people who lived prior to the flood had a very long lifespan. Some scientists hypothesize that a great mist surrounded the earth prior to the flood which filtered out the sun's harmful rays; harmful rays which scientists now know contribute to cancer, even aging. It's feasible that Noah heard from his grandfather, Methuselah, how Enoch had fellowshipped with God. God's thoughts were passed from Enoch, to Methuselah, to Lamech, to Noah. Enoch taught them how to hear God's voice.

According to the Bible, God took Enoch away from the earth about 69 years before Noah was born. Noah was born when his father Lamech was 182 years old. Noah's grandfather, Methuselah, was 369 years old when Noah was born. Methuselah died at the ripe old age of 969, living longer than even his son Lamech. So Methuselah had 600 years to teach Noah. He taught Lamech and Noah what he had learned about God from his father Enoch.

One thing certainly stands out which separates Enoch from the rest of mankind. The scriptures imply Enoch never had to face death. Even Jesus the Lamb of God had to suffer death for the sins of mankind. What can give a man such favor with God that he doesn't face death?

> For this is what the high and lofty One says—he who lives forever, whose name is holy: "I live in a high and holy place, but also with him who is contrite and lowly in spirit, to revive the spirit of the lowly and to revive the heart of the contrite."
> —Isaiah 57:15

God lives with those who have a humble and contrite spirit. Webster's dictionary defines contrite as "a repentant spirit; grieving and sorrow over sin or shortcomings." A contrite person is one who is willing to be corrected. Apparently, Enoch had an encounter with God, which changed his life. Enoch listened to God and heeded His words. He was willing to change and do whatever God told him to. From that time forth, Enoch fellowshipped regularly with God. Enoch became a God chaser. He esteemed fellowship with God above all else. As a result, Enoch attained a perfection very few have ever achieved.

> Once there was a man named Enoch who pleased God, and God loved him. While Enoch was still living among sinners, God took him away, so that evil and falsehood could not corrupt his mind and soul. (We all know that people can be so fascinated by evil that they cannot recognize what is good even when they are looking right at it. Innocent people can be so corrupted with desire that they can think of nothing but what they want.) This man Enoch achieved in a few years' time a perfection that other people could never attain in a complete lifetime. The Lord was pleased with Enoch's life and

quickly took him out of this wicked world. People were aware of his departure but didn't understand. They never seemed to learn the lesson that God is kind and merciful to his own people; he protects those whom he has chosen.[1]

—Wisdom of Solomon 4:10-15

Come Away with Me My Love

One who has known close fellowship with God can imagine how Enoch arose before dawn in anticipation. While the world was still asleep, Enoch would venture outside for his daily fellowship with God. All was quiet except for the sound of his footsteps. God's presence surrounded him like a warm blanket on a chilled frost morning. The Alpha and Omega was there, waiting to greet him. In the dawn's quietness, the Lord's still small voice could be heard with clarity. The judgment of the great flood hadn't until now descended upon the earth. The earth still had remnants of Eden's paradise.

The book of Genesis informs us there was no man to till the ground. But a great mist covered the earth, keeping the soil rich and moist (Genesis 2:5-6). Trees and plants grew to their full potential. There were no droughts or floods. God and Enoch enjoyed seeing the giant trees and plants, many which became extinct following the Great Flood. They smelled the beautiful flowers' wonderful fragrance. Enoch picked some of the luscious fruit, herbs, and nuts to eat along the way.

> I come to the garden alone,
> While the dew is still on the roses,
> And the voice I hear, falling on my ear,
> The Son of God discloses,
>
> And He walks with me, and He talks with me,
> And He tells me I am His own;
> And the joy we share as we tarry there,
> None other has ever known.
>
> He speaks, and the sound of his voice
> Is so sweet the birds hush their singing,
> And the melody that He gave to me,
> Within my heart is ringing,

And He walks with me, and He talks with me,
And He tells me I am His own;
And the joy we share as we tarry there,
None other has ever known.

I'd stay in the garden with Him
Though the night around me be falling,
But He bids me go; thro' the voice of woe
His voice to me is calling,

And He walks with me, and He talks with me,
And He tells me I am His own;
And the joy we share as we tarry there,
None other has ever known.[2]

A sweetness from another world enveloped Enoch; a time of reverence; walking on Holy ground. Enoch entered into a realm with God in which many never imagine. With little distraction, Enoch heard the crystal clear voice of his beloved Creator. God spoke to Enoch concerning truth and righteousness. Enoch received a vision of the coming Messiah (Jude 1:14-15). God revealed to him what it was like in heaven. He could sense God's great love; a love he had never known before, far above the imperfect love of men. Enoch was overwhelmed with God's gentleness and goodness. He found his Creator was also his most trusted friend, a friend who sticks closer than a brother (Pr. 18:24). Joy and peace filled him as he continued his daily walk with God.

Soon the birds began their singing, making melody unto their Creator. The first rays of light began to penetrate the canopy of mist which surrounded the earth. The brilliance of dawn arose as God and Enoch walked together. They saw the picturesque sky and agreed it was good. As this exhilarating scene faded into the morning, people began to emerge from their homes to start their daily routines, oblivious to Enoch's wonderful experience that had just transpired. God's manifested presence began to lift. Alas, the time had come for Enoch to begin his daily chores. A tinge of sadness filled his heart as he realized he must attend his responsibilities (Ps. 27:4).

Besides, this experience with God wasn't just for Enoch. God wanted Enoch to go and share his wonderful experience. He desired Enoch to tell of His excellent greatness. He commissioned Enoch to go and preach on repentance and righteousness. God not only wanted to fellowship with Enoch, but with all of mankind.

His family and servants waited for him. Everyone knew where he was; walking with the Creator.

Enoch deeply loved his wife and children. He was a hard worker; a good provider for his family; a wealthy man. He enjoyed the bountiful blessings of his home and livestock. Enoch delighted in serving others. But there is nothing to compare with God's manifested glory. The more you get to know God, the more you desire to know Him. Reluctantly, Enoch headed home.

God began to give Enoch visions and further revelation. Since Enoch was one who could be trusted, God began to reveal to him deeper truths. Many times Enoch was caught away in the spirit and shown things in the spiritual realm. He saw visions of the future and things to come (Jude 1:14-15).

As Enoch grew closer to God each year, I believe he reflected more and more of God's glory. His manner of speech, the compassion in his eyes, his unparalleled wisdom, his powerful preaching, all witnessed of his fellowship and authority with God. I believe when Enoch emerged from his time with God, his face radiated with God's glory, just as Moses had (Exodus 34:29).

Enoch also received much persecution because of his close fellowship with God. We know from examples in the Bible those who radiate such glory are subjected to much persecution from the world. Jesus said to His disciples,

> Blessed are those who are persecuted because of righteousness, for theirs is the kingdom of heaven. Blessed are you when people insult you, persecute you and falsely say all kinds of evil against you because of me. Rejoice and be glad, because great is your reward in heaven, for in the same way they persecuted the prophets who were before you.
> —Matthew 5:10-12

It seems the closer one gets to God, the more he is subjected to insults and ridicule. From the example of Jesus' ministry on earth, we know the most intense persecution comes from the religious—those who have a form of religion, but don't really know God. Although little is said concerning Enoch's life, we can surmise from the examples of other godly men and women throughout history that he suffered persecution.

If you are insulted because of the name of Christ, you are blessed, for the Spirit of glory and of God rests on you.

—1 Peter 4:14

But the persecution didn't shake Enoch. He had tasted of the heavenly manna. He had found a heavenly treasure and it was worth selling all he owned to obtain it. He had found a pearl more brilliant than any gem of this world (Matthew 13:44-46). So grand was this treasure, he was willing to endure any hardship to obtain it; he was willing to sacrifice all things to keep it. Enoch continued to fellowship with God and preach God's kingdom to all who'd listen. God enjoyed the fellowship of Enoch because He took him away from this earth into heaven.

We tend to fellowship with those whom we share things in common. When we fellowship with one another and become bonded together in unity, we begin to think more alike. Enoch began to hate sin and evil, just as God hates sin and evil. Enoch began to love righteousness, just as God loves righteousness. Enoch began to think the God-kind of thoughts. He refrained from anything unholy. He considered the poor and destitute. He showed his enemies kindness and forgiveness. Others noticed a difference in Enoch and his family. He didn't fit the mold of the world. He was holy, set apart by God.

Soon Enoch was teaching others about righteousness. God revealed to Enoch mysteries of the universe, heaven, His kingdom; mysteries concerning the future. Enoch taught his son, Methuselah. He also taught his grandson, Lamech. Methuselah and Lamech passed this righteousness to Noah, the righteousness that comes by faith. Noah followed in Enoch's footsteps. So Enoch's seed was preserved from judgment through Noah, his great-grandson. When we become preachers of righteousness through Jesus Christ, it will influence our children, grandchildren, and even our great-grandchildren. They will have greater opportunity to be spared from judgments to come, just as Noah was spared.

Enoch received visions and revelations concerning the second coming of Christ. Enoch warned of judgments to come. Enoch prophesied of the end times revealing how Jesus would come with His saints and execute judgment on the earth. He was a preacher of righteousness. Enoch tried to convince the wicked to repent and turn to God.

> Enoch, the seventh from Adam, prophesied about these men: "See, the Lord is coming with thousands upon thousands of his holy ones to judge everyone, and to convict all the ungodly of all the ungodly acts they have done in the ungodly way, and of all the harsh words ungodly sinners have spoken against him."
>
> —Jude 1:14-15

Enoch also spoke of salvation and forgiveness of sin. However, they refused to listen, just as they refused to listen to Noah. They questioned Enoch's authority, "Who gives you the right to be God's spokesperson? Who are you to judge us? We refuse to listen to your negative, doomsday preaching. You're just a mean spirited man. Do you think you're better than us?"

He knew what was good and righteous because he walked with God. Enoch was grieved with the evil of his generation. Each year, he seemed to withdraw more from his evil surroundings. He'd enter into the Holy of Holies to fellowship with God. He'd emerge again from God's presence to preach righteousness and to teach his children and grandchildren; all who'd listen. But his love for God always brought him back into the secret place of the Most High. God and Enoch were enjoying one another so much He decided to take Enoch away to be forever in His presence.

> By faith Enoch was taken from this life, so that he did not experience death; he could not be found, because God had taken him away. For before he was taken, he was commended as one who pleased God. And without faith it is impossible to please God, because anyone who comes to him must believe that he exists and that he rewards those who earnestly seek him.
>
> —Hebrews 11:5-6

Chapter 3

FAVOR WITH GOD

AS MENTIONED, NOAH grew up hearing about his great grandfather, Enoch, how he walked with God, and suddenly disappeared from the face of the earth because God took him. He heard from his grandfather, Methuselah, and his father, Lamech, about God's righteousness. By the time he was an adult, Noah was trained in God's ways. He knew God's voice and walked with God, much like his grandfather, Enoch.

God saw man's wickedness that covered the earth. Because the thoughts of man were continually evil, God regretted having created man. Men had gotten involved with hobbies, work and the world's cares. Mankind gradually drifted away and eventually forgot God.

When man's thoughts aren't filled with the knowledge of God, a spiritual void is created. Man is a spirit being and was created to worship, serve and fellowship with God. Accordingly, there is a hunger in man that can only be satisfied by our Creator. If man doesn't seek the Lord to fulfill this spiritual hunger, he will attempt to appease it with other things. He may look to other gods; to sex, parties, material wealth, or entertainment. These idols cannot gratify the deep inner longing of man's desire for God. He will always be left discontent and empty.

The Declaration of Independence states men have a right to life, liberty, and the pursuit of happiness. Alas, the truth is that life, liberty, and the pursuit of happiness are all elusive. Without God, there can be no life, liberty, nor happiness. True joy, freedom and contentment can only be found in Christ.

In pursuing happiness apart from God, mankind fell into the depths of darkness. God saw the wickedness of man and was sorry He had made them. Instead of choosing righteousness, men chose to do evil. Like many today, men were consumed with self-gratification.

Rather than pursuing happiness, Noah pursued God. Overcoming the world's distractions, Noah heard his beloved Creator's voice.

> So God said to Noah, "I am going to put an end to all people, for the earth is filled with violence because of them. I am surely going to destroy both them and the earth."
>
> —Genesis 6:13

God told Noah He was going to destroy all the people on the earth, even all the animals. Because God had given man dominion and authority over the earth, man influenced the earth for good or evil as seen in Genesis 1:28.

At this time when men were corrupting the earth, even the animals were corrupted with evil. Animals, as well as man, can be influenced by evil. Demons can actually possess animals. When Jesus was about to cast out the legion of demons from the man in the region of Gerasenes, the demons begged Jesus to send them into a nearby heard of swine. Jesus granted their request (Mark 5:1-13). It's possible pets can take on some characteristics of their masters, just as children can their parents. In Genesis 1:28 God gave man dominion over the earth. God commanded Adam and Eve to subdue it and to rule over the fish, the birds, and every living creature that moves on the ground. Consequently, we influence animals more than most of us realize.

When Israel entered the Promised Land, God gave them specific instructions for each region or group of people that they were to conquer. In some instances God told them to kill the men, but spare the women and children. On other occasions Israel's enemies were to be completely annihilated—men, women, children; even the animals. Sometimes God prohibited Joshua from taking any spoils of war. Could it be inanimate objects such as idols can also be possessed by demons?

God, Himself, hardened the hearts of Israel's enemies in order to remove the evil from the earth.

> Joshua waged war against all these kings for a long time. Except for the Hivites living in Gibeon, not one city made a treaty of peace with the Israelites, who took them all in battle. For it was the LORD himself who hardened their hearts to wage war against Israel, so that he might destroy them totally, exterminating them without mercy, as the LORD had commanded Moses.
>
> —Joshua 11:18-20

God then began to give Noah detailed instructions on how to build the ark. Noah was faced with a choice. He could believe God and act on His Word or he could stay in his comfort zone and perish. Perhaps he was overwhelmed at the magnitude of such a project. Nevertheless, Noah feared God more than he feared man. He believed what God had spoken. He took a step of faith and began to build the ark. Noah wasn't lazy. He wasn't a quitter. He was a diligent worker and persevered until the ark was completed. He obeyed and did all God commanded.

Noah, unlike the rest of his generation, was a man of righteousness. The Bible calls Noah a preacher of righteous. He warned of the judgment to come and God's provision of safety through the ark.

> For if God did not spare angels when they sinned, but sent them to hell, putting them into gloomy dungeons to be held for judgment; if he did not spare the ancient world when he brought the flood on its ungodly people, but protected Noah, a preacher of righteousness, and seven others; — if this is so, then the Lord knows how to rescue godly men from trials and to hold the unrighteous for the day of judgment, while continuing their punishment.
>
> —2 Peter 2:4-5, 9

God didn't spare the angels from judgment. He didn't spare Noah's generation, nor did He spare Sodom and Gomorrah. God was deeply grieved with mankind. God made these an example of what will eventually happen to all the ungodly that refuse to repent.

However, God chose to spare Noah and rescue him from judgment. Indeed, God knows how to rescue godly men when he brings judgment on the rest of mankind. Noah must have known God's righteousness because the Bible describes him as a preacher of righteousness. Noah was different from the rest of the world. Noah found grace in the Lord's eyes. What moved God to spare Noah and his family, as the rest of the world perished?

> This is the account of Noah. Noah was a righteous man, blameless among the people of his time, and he walked with God.
> —Genesis 6:9

Why did the Bible called Noah blameless when we know all have sinned and fallen short of God's glory (Rom. 3:23)? Just as his great-grandfather, Enoch, Noah walked with God. While the world was thinking about everything but God, Noah was consumed with God. While the rest of mankind was pursuing pleasure and happiness, Noah was pursuing God, listening to His voice. Because Noah pursued fellowship with God and obeyed by faith, he was called blameless by God. God spoke to him and showed him things to come. Then Noah believed God. Noah's heart was completely surrendered to God. Therefore, he was called just and perfect. Like Enoch, his great-grandfather, Noah had a personal relationship with God.

In reverence and the fear of God, Noah prepared an ark. Some scientists believe it had never before rained on the earth until the judgment of Noah's generation. The Bible seems to reinforce this theory.

> This is the account of the heavens and the earth when they were created. When the LORD God made the earth and the heavens— and no shrub of the field had yet appeared on the earth and no plant of the field had yet sprung up, for the LORD God had not sent rain on the earth and there was no man to work the ground, but streams came up from the earth and watered the whole surface of the ground— the LORD God formed the man from the dust of the ground and breathed into his nostrils the breath of life, and the man became a living being.
> —Genesis 2:4-7

My high school Chemistry teacher taught us his theory concerning the flood, which I've never forgotten. He taught us about the sun's alpha, beta, and gamma rays. Some of these rays are somewhat healthy. However, other rays may cause cancer and are a major cause of aging. Theoretically, if you could filter out the sun's harmful rays while allowing the healthy rays, you could virtually stop the aging process.

A fine mist covered the earth during the days before the flood, which filtered out many of the sun's harmful rays. According to the chemistry teacher, this explains why the people of Noah's day lived to be 800 and 900 years old. In addition, the plants didn't require as much work to yield its fruit because a mist watered the earth, keeping the soil moist and rich with minerals.

After the flood, there was no mist to filter the sun's harmful rays. Men had to do hard labor to till the ground. Life became much more difficult. There was a significant increase in bacteria, viruses, and diseases. After the flood God reduced man's lifespan. Each century, mankind's rebellion leads him further away from the paradise of Eden.

It's plausible that prior to the flood, no one had ever seen a thunderstorm. Still, Noah believed God and began building the ark, even though he was the only one who heard and believed.

Obedience and Perseverance

> By faith Noah, when warned about things not yet seen, in holy fear built an ark to save his family. By his faith he condemned the world and became heir of the righteousness that comes by faith.
> —Hebrews 11:7

Hebrews tells us Noah's steps of obedience condemned the rest of the world. Why did Noah's faith condemn the rest of the world? Because Noah believe God when others refused to believe. Not only did Noah believe, but he obeyed. It isn't enough just to believe. True faith will result in obedience. Faith hears God's voice and takes steps of action to obey. Noah could have heard God's voice, but refused to believe. He could have believed God when He told him of the flood, but refused to take the necessary steps to obey God and build the ark. What if Noah began to complain half way through building the ark?

"This is too hard, God. Are you sure I must build such a monumental structure? I'm tired. I underestimated the costs involved. It's more work than I expected. This is taking way too much time and energy. Perhaps judgment isn't coming after all. Maybe I just thought I heard God. I could have misunderstood. This is too difficult a task; I give up; I quit," he may have complained.

Had Noah given up, he'd have perished in the flood. But Noah worked until the ark was complete. He also persevered in preaching righteousness, warning of judgment to come. In His mercy God wanted to give all of mankind an opportunity to be saved. Noah possibly hired people to help him build the ark. Noah, himself, also endured back breaking work; his obedience subjected him to the unbelievers' ridicule. Nevertheless, by faith, he finished the job. His obedience saved his family from destruction.

> Then the LORD said, "My Spirit will not contend with man forever, for he is mortal; his days will be a hundred and twenty years."
> —Genesis 6:3

This wicked generation had the same opportunity as Noah. They could have walked with God; believed the preaching of Noah, repented, and helped him build the ark. They had an opportunity before it began raining to enter the ark's safety. In spite of that, they refused. Their evil unbelief condemned them to perish. Unbelief is perhaps the greatest sin. It destroyed the Hebrew children in the wilderness. It resulted in the Pharisees crucifying Jesus. It will keep us from entering into God's promises.

Unbelief will keep one in bondage to the heavy yoke of sin. It leads to deception. Once deceived, we are subject to Satan's bidding. This cornerstone of truth exists throughout the ages. Many of this present generation will be condemned because they refuse to believe the truth. Noah's faith and obedience was counted as righteousness.

> The LORD then said to Noah, "Go into the ark, you and your whole family, because I have found you righteous in this generation."
> —Genesis 7:1

Today, Christ is extending an invitation to those who have surrendered their lives to Him, "Come you and your entire house

into the ark; for you have been made righteous by your faith in Me"
(2 Corinthians 5:21).

Obedience Brings Persecution

Just as many of our generation dishonor preachers of righteousness,
Noah's generation most certainly contended with Noah. They questioned his authority, "What makes you so special to think you know
God? You speak of strange things we've never heard before. Do you
really believe water will fall from the sky? You're just a crazy old man; a
negative, doomsday preacher. God would never destroy His creation!"

I'm sure some became very angry with Noah. They threatened Noah
and his family for exposing their darkness. Some probably accused him
of being judgmental. Others mocked him in their unbelief. Noah had to
battle doubt. He probably thought, "How can I be right and everyone
else wrong?" Could it be few will hear the Lord's voice at the time of
His coming as in the days of Noah?

> Enter through the narrow gate. For wide is the gate and broad is the
> road that leads to destruction, and many enter through it. But small is
> the gate and narrow the road that leads to life and only a few find it.
> —Matthew 7:13-14

When I was a young man, I had a shirt with an imprint on it. It
showed a flowing stream with many fish. All of the fish were flowing
downstream except for one lonely, brave fish. Unlike the others, he was
swimming upstream. A Bible verse on the shirt read,

> Do not conform any longer to the pattern of this world, but be
> transformed by the renewing of your mind. Then you will be able to
> test and approve what God's will is—his good, pleasing and perfect
> will.
> —Romans 12:2

It's easy to flow downstream with all the other fish. It requires less
work and is more comfortable. Most people just go with the flow; "que
sera, sera, whatever will be, will be." It takes courage and determination

to swim upstream. You will stand out as being different and strange. Some will make fun of you and label you a fanatic. The truth is everyone is a fanatic about something. Some love sports, jobs, or movies. The list continues. What do you think and talk about the most? This is what you love, what is in your heart. This is what or whom you worship.

Jesus said that at the time of His return, the world would be like the days of Noah. In the days of Noah, lawlessness and violence filled the earth, just as it is today. In our present generation, men's hearts have become cold, hard, and even cruel. Many are arrogant, refusing to receive the truth of God's Word. They are lovers of themselves; lovers of pleasure more than lovers of God (2 Timothy 3:2-5).

The few men and women who warn of judgment and repentance are often met by criticism, contempt, and ridicule. The nonbelievers respond to their preaching with threats and anger. Those who preach the truth are despised, rejected, and at best ignored by most of the world. The modern day preachers of righteousness face hostility and dishonor, even from those within the Church. Some who don't say anything outwardly still display their true feelings by being cold and indifferent toward them, treating them almost as an outcast; someone with a plague.

Many popular ministers are afraid to be seen with them, fearing reprisal from their congregations and those who support their ministry. Nonetheless, these brave preachers continue to preach the message God has burned in their hearts; the message of repentance and salvation through Jesus Christ; the warning of impending judgment upon those who refuse to repent; the good news that Jesus is preparing His bride for His soon return.

Is it possible that most of the world, even those who attend church, will be deceived into taking the mark of the beast? I believe only a small group which Jesus refers to as the elect will be saved when Christ returns, just as only a few were saved from the great flood of Noah's generation when Noah continually warned of the judgment to come (Matthew 24:24).

Yes, many reject these preachers of righteousness and their message just as the people did Noah, in his generation. And yet, time marches on toward the final countdown to Armageddon. Those who believe, as well as those who refuse to believe, will see these things come to pass.

Notice in Hebrews 11:7, where the Holy Scripture says Noah prepared an ark by which he condemned the world. God has given everyone the privilege of choice. Noah preached for 120 years during the time he was preparing the ark. Everyone had the same opportunity to be saved as did Noah, but he or she chose to ignore God's Word. They probably thought, "There he goes again. Noah has been preaching this for a hundred years and where is the judgment he has spoken of?" Some may have believed at the beginning. But as the years passed, they began to doubt. Eventually they became entangled with the world's cares and the deceitfulness of riches (Matthew 13:18-23).

Suddenly, like a thief in the night, the rain began to pour from above and the water gushed from beneath. But Noah had heard God's voice and was prepared. He and his family were safe and dry. God shut the ark's doors. After many years of striving with men to change their evil ways, the final curtain closed on His mercy.

So shall it be with the Lord's coming. God has warned through His prophets. In His mercy God will continue to warn right up to the final day. He will give the world plenty of time to prepare for His coming. But when it doesn't occur speedily, they will doubt, lose interest, and become entangled with the world's cares. Suddenly, like a thief in the night, the Messiah will come.

I'm often amused with how the news media exploits false prophecies which predict the day or year for the end of the age. Jesus says, "No one knows about that day or hour, not even the angels in heaven, nor the Son, but only the Father" (Matthew 24:36). If the angels of heaven and Jesus Himself don't know the day of His coming, how can a so called prophet know?

If we hear news media hype about a year or day for which the world ends such as Y2K, May 21st, 2011, Nostradamus, or the 2012 Mayan Calendar, we can rest assured, it a false prediction. When Christ returns it will take the news media, indeed the whole world by surprise.

Jesus said He'd return suddenly like a thief in the night (Luke 12:35-40). Notice Jesus said he'd return like a thief in the night for *those who aren't ready*. Who are the unprepared? Those who don't have their lamps filled with oil (Matthew 25:1-13). Oil is often used in the Bible to symbolize the Holy Spirit. In other words, those who aren't watching and waiting on God; those who are lazy, hiding their God given talents; those more concerned with the world's cares than with God's kingdom; those who aren't full of the Holy Spirit.

For those who stay close to the Vine (Jesus), they will discern the signs of the times. They will have their lamps full of oil and will be ready. These virgins will hear the voice of the trumpet. They will be spared those terrible days of judgment which will fall upon the earth. Just as in the days of Noah, the final curtain of mercy will draw shut, but those whose lamps are filled with oil will be safe inside the Ark, which is a type of Christ Jesus. Will you be ready?

Once the ark's door was shut, the rains came; spouts of water coming from within the earth and a pouring down from above. Every living thing that moved upon the earth perished. Everything on dry land drowned. Death covered the whole land, except for the ark. Only Noah was left and those with him in the ark. The waters flooded the earth for a hundred and fifty days. The Bible says God remembered Noah and sent a great wind so the waters receded. Then God said, "Come out of the ark, you and those with you. Bring out all the animals so they can crawl upon the ground."

To show his thankfulness for God's mercy toward him, Noah built an altar and offered sacrifices on it. God was pleased with Noah's grateful act and promised He'd never destroy all the creatures again with a flood. He set a rainbow in the clouds as a sign of His promise to men, a promise to Noah, the preacher of righteousness, and to all his descendants. Just as God sent a rainbow of promise in the clouds, He sent His Son of promise on the cross that those who believe on Him might be saved.

After God's judgment, comes restoration. Just as God restored the earth after the flood, he will restore the earth after the great tribulation. God will send His Son to save the earth from man's destruction and restore all things. He will come again to reign forever from Jerusalem. He will rule in righteousness. He will show mercy to men and animals, restoring the earth to the most marvelous state since the Garden of Eden. Will you be there in His righteous kingdom?

Chapter 4

THE SPIRIT OF ELIJAH

DARK TIMES HAD come upon the land of Israel. Most had fallen into idolatry. Prostitution was at an all time high. Jezebel, the evil wife of King Ahab, had influenced much of Israel to abandon Jehovah and worship Baal instead. Ahab built a temple and set up an altar for Baal. He provoked the God of Israel to anger. The nation had all but forgotten their covenant with God. Some thought they could serve other gods as well as Jehovah the living God.

But God was preparing a man for such a time as this. God anointed a man named Elijah to stem the evil tide in Israel. Unlike other great men of the Bible no information is given about Elijah's birth and early childhood. But we can surmise from how God works with men that He groomed and trained Elijah from birth for his divine destiny.

A rugged individual with fur clothes and a leather belt around his waist, Elijah suddenly appears on the scene during some of the darkest times for Israel. Like Enoch and Noah, Elijah walked with God. Rising above the distractions of his day he heard God's voice. Soon he began to think like God. He stood bold and brave against the wickedness of his generation. He hated evil and loved justice, mercy, and righteousness. He was jealous for God's people. He sensed God's anger and sadness over the deteriorated condition of Israel. Elijah became a preacher of righteousness.

Out of Israel's millions of inhabitants only 7,000 people still hadn't bowed to Baal. Baal is a symbol of sensuality, pleasure, and entertainment. Could this be a type of what is to come at the end of days when most of the world will receive the Beast's mark?

America as a nation has fallen into idolatry, bowing to the idols of sex, rock music, entertainment, sports, and materialism. Much of America has bowed down and kissed the idol of self-gratification just as Israel had done during Elijah's lifetime. Hollywood entertainment, video games, sports, gambling casinos, partying, rock music, and abortion have become relatives of Baal. While not all of the entertainment industry is evil, it has become an idol to many in America. There are those in America who faithfully attend worship services at the arena or stadium each week, but seldom attend a church to worship God. Some faithfully watch their favorite television program, but never have time for daily devotion to God. Others spend much of their income at the casinos while robbing God by refusing to give Him their tithes and offerings.

Young people raise their arms and clap their hands as they worship their favorite rock star. At the same time, they show disrespect toward God and regard God's holy commandments with contempt and disdain. For some, life is a party with no concern for God or neighbor.

Others spend all their time and energy trying to obtain wealth. Every day they bow their knees to the God of status and material wealth. They are driven by pride and greed. Some would even sell their children to obtain the coveted wealth, status and power.

Young men and women commit fornication. They worship convenience and sexual gratification. When pregnancy occurs the young men refuse to take responsibility. For the love of money, doctors abort babies in the name of medical science. Consequently, they sacrifice their babies through legalized abortion, just as ancient Israel sacrificed their infants to Baal.

Nevertheless, God is still in control, just as He was during the days of Elijah. There were seven thousand in Israel who refused to bow to Baal. Likewise, there is a remnant in America who hasn't bowed to the idols of pleasure, entertainment, and self-gratification. These believers have kept their garments white, unstained by the world's sensuality. Their spiritual senses haven't become dull. They are able to discern the truth. This holy remnant can discern what is good and evil. To these people of

God, there is no uncertainty or gray areas, but light vs. darkness, black and white. God is the same yesterday, today and forever (Hebrews 13:8). The Bible is just as relevant today as when holy men of old were inspired to pen its words. The Holy One is raising modern day prophets with Elijah's mantle to call the nations to repentance.

Unlike the United States, Israel wasn't a democratic nation. Many times those who were most brutal would overthrow the weaker kings and rule instead. Most people of ancient Israel were probably afraid to do anything about the corrupt kings or didn't know how. They couldn't vote the evil kings out so they submitted to their evil influence. Israel's uncleanness resulted in broken fellowship with God. God withdrew His presence from the nation of Israel. Without God's presence for divine protection, Israel became vulnerable to her enemies.

The Man of God Appears

But there was one man who had a different spirit. Suddenly Elijah appears on the scene. He obtained an audience with Ahab, boldly proclaiming the Word of the Lord. How interesting that although Ahab was an evil king and worshipped other gods, he recognized Elijah as a prophet of the true God, the God of Abraham, Isaac, and Jacob. Perhaps out of curiosity and because he recognized Elijah's authority, he gave weight to Elijah's words. Maybe he had witnessed firsthand the miracles performed by Elijah. For whatever reason, King Ahab gave Elijah access to speak in his presence and listened to what he had to say.

Upon receiving direction from the Lord, Elijah approached King Ahab and boldly proclaimed, "As the Lord, the God of Israel, lives, whom I serve, there will be neither dew nor rain in the next few years except at my word." As word traveled of Elijah's bold declaration, the whole nation waited to see if his words would come to pass. Was he one just pretending to hear from God? Was he vying for power and political clout? Was he coveting fame and prestige, or was he really God's true prophet?

Meanwhile, the Word of the Lord came to Elijah, "Leave here, turn eastward and hide in the Kerith Ravine, east of the Jordan. You will drink from the brook and I have ordered the ravens to feed you there." By now Elijah had become so well trained in hearing God's voice and obeying by faith, he had no doubt or hesitation. He immediately left for the Kerith Ravine. The ravens served him morning and evening meals just as God promised. Elijah had bread and meat for his meals while he drank from the brook. God sent Elijah to the Kerith Ravine to protect his life from the famine. Perhaps when Israel's judgment began, some would seek to harm Elijah. God had Elijah's back covered. God, Himself, would back up the prophet Elijah.

As the months went by with no rain, it became evident Elijah's words had come true. As the drought continued, even the brook which supplied him with water dried up. Elijah refused to fret, but listened to hear God's voice of instruction. Then a Word from the Lord came to him, "Go at once to Zarephath of Sidon and stay there. I have commanded a widow there to supply you with food." Notice how God told Elijah that He had commanded a widow in Sidon to supply him with food. Thus, we know the widow of Zarephath could hear God's voice, but would she believe? By faith Elijah left the Kerith Ravine toward Zarephath having no knowledge of the widow's identity, where she lived, or how to find her. But he was confident God would guide him.

Elijah had been held in contempt among his own people in Israel. So for his protection, God sent him, not to a distinguished nobleman or wealthy Israeli citizen, but to a widow; a foreigner in Sidon. Elijah's own people dishonored him, so God sent him to a poor widow woman in Sidon who didn't have enough to support herself, much less Elijah. Jesus mentioned this when speaking at His hometown of Nazareth. His hometown dishonored and rejected Him just as Israel did Elijah.

> "I tell you the truth," he continued, "No prophet is accepted in his hometown. I assure you that there were many widows in Israel in Elijah's time, when the sky was shut for three and a half years and there was a severe famine throughout the land. Yet Elijah was not sent to any of them, but to a widow in Zarephath in the region of Sidon.
> —Luke 4:24-26

Elijah approached Zarephath dusty, tired, and thirsty. When he arrived at the town gate, he saw a lady gathering sticks. He knew she must be the one to whom God had sent him. But would she know? Would she recognize him as one whom God sent? Would she believe?

He called to her and asked, "Would you give me a little water in a jar so I may have a drink?" He felt somewhat relieved when she left to get him a drink. As she was going, he called, "Bring me a piece of bread, please."

Having recognized Elijah as God's prophet, she replied, "As surely as the LORD your God lives, I don't have any bread—only a handful of flour in a jar and a little oil in a jug. I am gathering a few sticks to take home and make a meal for myself and my son, that we may eat it—and die."

Elijah wasn't moved by the widow's discouragement. Indeed, while dread covered the land, Elijah could walk in peace and assurance. Having fellowshipped with God daily, he could never doubt God's love and faithfulness. He knew God would never leave him nor forsake him (Matthew 28:20). They were in covenant together. He had heard God's voice and obeyed His instructions. God said there was a widow at Zarephath who'd sustain him and Elijah believed God's Word. The One who guides will provide. God wouldn't send him to someone who'd reject him. If God trusted the character of this widow enough to send him to her, she must have faith in God and His prophet.

He said to the widow, "Don't be afraid. Go and prepare the meal. But first, make a small cake for me from what you have. Then make something for yourself and your son. For this is what the Lord, the God of Israel, says: 'The jar of flour will not be used up and the jug of oil will not run dry until the day the Lord gives rain on the land.'" The widow believed God and His preacher of righteousness. She became Abraham's seed by faith. She entered into Abraham's covenant with God; the covenant of faith. God chose this woman of Sidon to feed His prophet rather than anyone in the house of Israel. God sees into the heart. He saw in this widow a heart of great faith. She did as Elijah instructed and there was food everyday for Elijah, the woman, and her family.

Later, the woman's boy became ill and died. God used Elijah to raise him back to life. The blessing of Elijah, the preacher of righteousness, was upon the widow's house (Matthew 10:41). Because the woman believed Elijah and received him, it was counted to her as righteousness.

The Blame Game

Still many in Israel refused to believe that God was judging their nation, even though it hadn't rained for three and a half years. Many refused to believe Elijah's God was the one true God. Others were deceived into thinking they could worship Baal and Jehovah simultaneously. They reverenced Baal more than God. They feared Jezebel's words more than Elijah's. To them, the drought was nothing more than a natural phenomenon, nature running her course. King Ahab and Jezebel blamed it on Elijah, the doomsday preacher.

God was going to prove the drought resulted from His displeasure with Israel. God's Word came to Elijah, "Go and present yourself to Ahab and I will send rain on the land."

When King Ahab saw Elijah, he said, "Is that you troublemaker of Israel?"

"I haven't made trouble for Israel," Elijah replied. "But you and your father's family have. You have abandoned the Lord's commands and have followed the Baal."

Notice how King Ahab perceived Elijah as the one responsible for the nation's drought. Elijah was simply God's spokesperson. He just revealed to the people why Israel was facing such devastating problems. Elijah wasn't the cause of these problems, but was part of the solution. God wanted to use the prophet to return the nation to its glorious past. But when the prophet presented God's demands, many rejected the prophet. They weren't rejecting Elijah, but the One whom he represented. They'd rather worship their idols and participate in darkness even if it meant the destruction of Israel.

Some in our nation blame it's woes on right wing Christians who believe the Bible as God's inspired Word. But it isn't the Christians who have brought troubles upon this nation, but those who refuse to obey God's commandments, as taught in the Holy Scriptures; those in churches, government, education, Wall Street, and the entertainment industry who worship other gods. Their unwise choices have brought this nation to the brink of ruin. They disrespect God and His commandments. Jesus said, "If you love me, you will keep my commandments" (John 14:15).

Some blame our nation's problems on the liberals, while refusing to consider the poor, downtrodden and hopeless. Like Cain, they ask, "Am I my brother's keeper?" They are trapped in the materialism of this world and can't see beyond their life of comfort and ease. They look with disdain at the poor common man while chasing their vanities of power and wealth which can never satisfy. Ensnared with greed, they end up chasing the wind (Ecclesiastes 1:14).

As the preacher of Ecclesiastes says, "There's nothing new under the sun" (Ecclesiastes 1:9). These pitfalls are nothing new. Elijah confronted similar problems as those of today; self-worship, greed, idolatry, sexual perversions, unbelief, disrespect toward God and His commandments, the sacrificing of infants to idols.

Today, preachers of righteousness are labeled as troublemakers, sowing strife and discord within the church. But it isn't these men and women of God who are causing division, but God's truth as revealed in the Bible. Jesus said, "I come not to bring peace, but a sword" (Matthew 10:34-36). It isn't the preachers of righteousness who are troublemakers, but those who refuse to receive the truth. Yes, we're to pursue peace, but not at the expense of compromising the truth.

Elijah instructed King Ahab, "Now summon the people from all over Israel to meet me on Mount Carmel. And bring Baal's four hundred and fifty prophets and Asherah's four hundred prophets, who eat at Jezebel's table."

Ahab believed Elijah was a prophet. He knew there was power in Elijah's words and respected his word. So Ahab sent word throughout all Israel and assembled the prophets on Mount Carmel. Through Elijah, the Almighty brought Israel to the valley of decision. Elijah challenged Baal's priests and called all of the people to a town meeting. The preacher of righteousness declared, "The God who sends fire from heaven to consume the sacrifice is the true God."

Baal's prophets approached their altars and prayed to their god with no results. Hundreds of them called on the name of Baal from morning until noon, but not a sound. They cried out, "Baal, answer us!" But no one answered. They did their heathen dance around the altar they had made.

"Shout loudly, for he's a god! Maybe he's thinking it over; maybe he has wandered away; or maybe he is traveling the road on vacation. Perhaps he's sleeping and will wake up! Perhaps he is using the toilet." Elijah mused. They even cut their arms until they bled, according to their custom of worship. Still, there was only silence. They kept on begging until evening, but no response.

Repair the Altar

God had instructed Elijah to build an altar and place an offering on the altar. Then Elijah said to all the people, "Come near me." All the people approached him. They looked on as he repaired the Lord's altar that had been torn down.

The Lord's altar needs repairing in the United States and Western Europe. In these nations, leaders disregard God and the Bible. These nations, once strong in faith, have departed from God's ways. Even many who go to church and claim to be Christians don't really know Christ or His ways. They've never repented with godly sorrow. There's never been a change in their lifestyle. Because they love darkness rather than light, they deny the Gospel's power to deliver from sin. They carefully examine every true believer's life looking for some fault to discredit the Gospel's power.

Let's repair the Lord's altar; return to the Lord with weeping and repentance; return to God's altar of holiness, examining our hearts through the Holy Bible. Let's pray as David, "Create in me a clean heart O God. And renew a right spirit within me" (Psalm 51:10). Many want God's benefits of healing, blessings, and material prosperity. Still they're unwilling to come to God's altar. They're unwilling to endure the process of brokenness which leads to true repentance. Let's turn from shallow commitment and abandon ourselves to serve the living, risen, Savior.

Where is the Elijah who'll confront the idols of this generation? Where is the Elijah who'll demand change? Where is the Elijah who'll fear no man or devil? Where is the Elijah who asks, "How long will you waver between opinions? If God is God, then obey His Word! If God is God, then leave your idols!" Where is the Elijah who'll repair the altar?

Let's repair the altar and turn from iniquity. Let's return to our fathers' faith; those who founded this great nation; the puritans and pilgrims who first settled this nation. Theirs was a pure faith. They studied the Bible and believed. Not only did they believe, but they practiced their faith. They lived the Bible before their generation. They created laws based upon the Bible, laws which benefited society for generations to come. They exhibited good fruit such as discipline, charity, and hard work. They shared their faith with others unashamedly.

They were persecuted in Europe for their belief in the Bible; persecuted because their faith was more than just a religion, but a relationship with Christ; persecuted because their lives stood apart from the others as holy unto God. They fled the persecution of Europe for their right to worship Christ and study the scriptures.

Now, in the land of the free, true believers are once again being persecuted. But where can we go? There is no New World to flee to and start a new beginning. Let's stand up to the evils of today just as Elijah, and repair the Lord's altar.

Elijah took twelve stones according to the number of tribes in Israel and built an altar in the name of Yahweh. He instructed some men to dig a trench around the altar. He arranged the wood, cut up the bull and placed it on the wood. He instructed them to pour water on the altar three times as an act of faith. So the altar was drenched; water running all around the altar.

> Elijah went before the people and said, "How long will you waver between two opinions? If the LORD is God, follow him; but if Baal is God, follow him." But the people said nothing.
> —1 Kings 18:21

Those who don't spend time with God in His Word tend to waver in their thinking and opinions. Such was the case in Israel. The people formed their opinions based on who was in power, according to the popular opinion at the time. They didn't know God's ways because they never spent time in prayer, worship, or studying the scriptures. Similarly, many in America waver when it comes to important issues such as abortion, justice, prayer in schools, and voting for the right leaders. They have little knowledge of God's Word. They are unskilled in righteousness. Therefore, they aren't able to discern right from wrong. They are tossed to and fro in their opinions, like a fallen leaf on a windy autumn day. There is no certainty in their lives, no absolutes.

There are some who attend church services regularly, having little knowledge of the Bible. They hear what their pastor preaches or what some television show teaches. However, there are ministers who spend little time in prayer or the study of scriptures. All too often we as ministers get so busy "ministering," we fail to spend time in God's Word and in prayer. Sometimes we as ministers today spend our time serving congregations, networking with other ministers, and promoting our ministry, but have little quality time with God.

We end up with shallow teaching within the church instead of the meat of God's Word. The early Apostles made it a priority to avoid the trap of busyness.

> In those days when the number of disciples was increasing, the Grecian Jews among them complained against the Hebraic Jews because their widows were being overlooked in the daily distribution of food. So the Twelve gathered all the disciples together and said, "It would not be right for us to neglect the ministry of the word of God in order to wait on tables. Brothers, choose seven men from among you who are known to be full of the Spirit and wisdom. We will turn this responsibility over to them and will give our attention to prayer and the ministry of the word."
>
> —Acts 6:1-4

So the people of Elijah's day had little knowledge of the Holy Bible. They were too busy worshiping their gods. Keep in mind this was Israel, God's covenant people. Some may have known the scriptures, but didn't believe them. They did what was right in their own eyes.

The attitude toward God and His commandments were similar to that of today. Ministers who fear the opinions of men teach only on limited portions of the Bible, carefully avoiding correction and rebuke which are mentioned throughout the scriptures.

Like today idolatry was rampant. People showed contempt for those who stood up for righteousness. However, the man of God came on the scene and popular opinion was about to change. Elijah defended the Most High with holy boldness. Elijah took a stand against Israel's corruption, even at the risk of his life.

He preached with signs and wonders following. God was faithful to back up this preacher of righteousness. To assure the people this wasn't some magician's trick, Elijah soaked the offering not once, not twice, but three times with water so the water filled the trench. Water was everywhere, making it impossible to start a fire.

There was an eerie silence among the crowd as Elijah approached the altar and said, "Lord God of Abraham, Isaac, and Israel, today let it be known you are God in Israel and I am your servant, and at your word, I have done all these things. Answer me Lord! Answer me so this people will know You, Yahweh, are God and you have turned their hearts back."

Suddenly as a flash of lightening, fire from heaven consumed the offering. God desired to thoroughly convince His people. Not only was the bull consumed by the fire, but the wood, the stones, and even the dust were consumed. The fire licked up all the water in the trench. The people were overwhelmed with this awesome display of power. The fear of God came upon the people and they fell down on their faces crying out, "The Lord, He is God!"

They were no longer wavering in their opinions. At least for the time being, the people were convinced Jehovah, whom Elijah served was God.

Similarly in the United States, people seem to change their opinions with each election. They vote leaders into office who have no knowledge of the Bible and God's Spirit. These leaders succumb to the pressure of special interest groups who support ungodly agendas such as homosexual rights, Hollywood values, pro abortion, greedy corporations, and hostile foreign governments.

When God's judgment comes upon the nation, people begin to realize the nation is no longer prospering. Once again the people vote righteous leaders into office who enact just laws and work for the people's good. As they turn back to God in repentance, God demonstrates His power and restores the nation's prosperity.

Once the Lord's altar is rebuilt and an offering of commitment given in our nation, God will display His awesome power. When God's altar is rebuilt He will once again heal, restore, and pour out His blessings upon this nation. When we with godly sorrow return to God's altar, our faith will be renewed and restored. We can have confidence with God. We can experience a great revival as our forefathers before us.

Elijah ordered them, "Seize the prophets of Baal! Don't let even one of them escape." He had hundreds of Baal's priests executed. Like Elijah, church leaders must put to death the false gods of America. We must put to death the current error in doctrine that leads to lawlessness. Jesus loves us even when we are sinners. But He doesn't want us to remain sinners.

False conversions have occurred in recent generations; those who have a mental consent Jesus is God's Son, but have never truly repented or appropriated His righteousness by faith. They profess to be Christians, but their lives remain unchanged. They refuse to surrender their will to Jesus Christ; refuse to make Him Lord of their lives. Because of unbelief, they have never partaken of God's divine nature by faith. God expects us to come to Him in repentance. He expects us to overcome by faith exhibiting the character of Christ. This is the evidence of true conversion.

> By their fruit you will recognize them. Do people pick grapes from thorn bushes, or figs from thistles? Likewise every good tree bears good fruit, but a bad tree bears bad fruit. A good tree cannot bear bad fruit, and a bad tree cannot bear good fruit.
> —Matthew 7:16-18

Grace demands change. Let's put to death the sin in our lives and walk in newness of life; put to death the idols of our nation, just as Elijah put to death Baal's prophets.

God's Mercy Brings Rain

Elijah said to King Ahab, "Go eat and drink, for there is the sound of a rainstorm." Elijah was implying to Ahab, "The day of famine, fasting, and judgment is over. God's judgment has been delayed for now. Go eat, drink, and celebrate. For God has forgiven the nation. He has given you the benefit of the doubt. He has confidence you will put away your idols and love Him with all of your heart."

While Ahab went up to eat and drink, Elijah went up to Mount Carmel's summit. He bowed down, put his face between his knees, and prayed. Then he said to his servant, "Go up and look toward the sea." The servant came back and said, "There is nothing." Seven times Elijah prayed and the servant looked for the rain clouds.

Many may have given up in unbelief after the first time spent in prayer. They may have given up on their loved ones or their nation to ever change. Some may reason within their hearts, *God has failed me. I must have missed God. Why would God allow this to happen? He told me to get ready for rain and there is no rain. I prayed for the rain, but nothing.* But Elijah didn't give up. He persevered in prayer. Sometimes, we give up too quickly. If we just continue to pray in faith, the rain will come. In some instances God's people are at the threshold of breakthroughs, but give up. Like the Hebrews in the wilderness, they fail to enter into the promised land.

But Elijah had the Spirit of faith, the same spirit which was in Joshua and Caleb. On the seventh time, the servant reported, "There's a small cloud about the size of a hand coming from the sea." That's what Elijah was waiting to hear.

Elijah said to his servant, "Go and tell Ahab, 'Get your chariot ready and go to Jezreel immediately so the rain doesn't stop you.'" God's power came upon Elijah and he ran ahead of Ahab to Jezreel, outrunning Ahab's chariot. God will go to great lengths to assist those who stand for His truth and believe in Him.

Elijah was just an ordinary person like you and I; an ordinary person who served an extraordinary God. He trusted God to hear his prayers. Elijah knew the authority God had given him. He exercised his authority to change a nation.

> The prayer of a righteous man is powerful and effective. Elijah was a man just like us. He prayed earnestly that it would not rain, and it did not rain on the land for three and a half years. Again he prayed, and the heavens gave rain, and the earth produced its crops.
> —James 5:14-18

James describes the power of a righteous man's prayers by using this example of Elijah. Elijah was a man of great faith. He listened to God's voice and obeyed. That's why his prayers could control the weather.

Elijah abided in the Lord and meditated on God's Word. Accordingly, God placed His desires within Elijah's heart. God had a plan to bring a nation back to Him. So when Elijah prayed for it to stop raining, he was following God's plan.

Similarly, God has a plan to bring America back to Him. He will reveal it to His intercessors, just as He did Elijah. God's love has been rejected, His grace abused. His last resort will be to bring judgments at different times, locations, and various degrees, leading America to repentance.

As believers we have authority on this earth. We can pray with the same faith of Elijah and expect results. We can pray for our nation to turn back to God and be spared from judgment. Our prayers can bring the rain promised in Joel 2:23. The fervent prayers of a small remnant can spark the fires of revival and change a nation.

Through prayer, Elijah demonstrated God's mighty power. Elijah may have thought that surely this demonstration of power would change Ahab and Jezebel's hearts. They would respect him and put away their idols. But instead, the execution of Baal's priests made the evil queen Jezebel furious. Even after this great demonstration of power, she still denied Elijah's authority and vowed to have him executed, just as her priests were executed. Upon hearing this, Elijah became disappointed and dejected. The anointing had somewhat lifted and all he could see was himself, an ordinary man. Elijah had challenged a whole nation. In the process he became tired and weary.

"How much longer must I deal with this wicked queen?" he sighed. From Beersheba, he went a day's journey into the desert until he came to a broom tree. There, he sat down and prayed to die.

"I have had enough, LORD," he said. "Take my life; I am no better than my ancestors." Having said this he lay under the tree and fell asleep.

In spite of this, God had patience toward Elijah and sent an angel to strengthen him and restore his confidence. Strengthened by the angel's food, he traveled forty days and forty nights until he reached Mt. Horeb, God's mountain; a place of refuge and safety. There he went into a cave and spent the night.

In the cave, God spoke to him, "What are you doing here, Elijah?" Elijah was running from Queen Jezebel's wrath. God didn't intend for him to hide in the cave, but to finish his assigned job; to bring Israel back to truth.

Elijah replied, "I have been zealous for the Lord. The Israelites have broken your covenant, torn down your altars, and put your prophets to death. I am the only one left, and now they're trying to kill me too."

The Lord said, "Go out and stand on the mountain in My presence, for I am about to pass by." As Elijah stood on the mountain there was a great and powerful wind, followed by an earthquake and fire. But God wasn't in any of them. After the wind, earthquake, and fire, everything became quiet. In the stillness came a gentle whisper, "What are you doing here, Elijah?" God speaks, not in spectacular demonstrations; but in gentle whispers; in the quiet solitude of prayer. Just as God spoke to Enoch in the dawn's stillness; just as He spoke to Noah to build an ark; He spoke to Elijah in a still small voice.

Again Elijah replied, "I have been zealous for the Lord. The Israelites have broken your covenant, torn down your altars, and put your prophets to death. I am the only one left, and now they're trying to kill me too."

Sometimes, the negative news around us seems to overshadow God's goodness. In discouragement we sometimes focus on our negative circumstances. The deceiver tries to make things appear worse than they really are. Often in the midst of our suffering we feel helpless and alone.

Leaven in God's House

As a matter of fact there were 7,000 people in Israel who hadn't bowed to Baal. Similarly, there is a remnant in America who has stayed clear from the pollution which has contaminated the church. Nevertheless, some of the church in America is stained with the world. Let's take a side journey and look back in history to see how this occurred.

When President Jimmy Carter came into office in 1976, he made a public statement that he was a born again Christian. He was one of the first presidents of modern times who spoke of being "born again." The news media picked up on his statement. Christians in the United States received the news media's attention. President Carter stressed the need for compassion by helping the poor and bringing attention to those being persecuted in other nations for political or religious reasons. He pushed a foreign policy emphasizing human rights. America began to focus more on those who were persecuted in Eastern Europe, China, and the Soviet Union. The church began to intercede for these nations. As they interceded, they felt a connection with believers behind the iron curtain. They felt God's heart for the suffering within these nations. The people of these nations hungered for freedom.

The media sensed something unusual was taking place and began to ask questions about the born again experience. New inroads were made in preaching the gospel. Billy Graham gained new found prominence and respect. Ronald Reagan followed with his strong faith and character. Soon, being a Christian became popular. Sports figures proclaimed their faith in Christ. Celebrities began appearing on various Christian television programs. A Christian renewal occurred in the late 1970's and 1980's. God's Spirit emphasized faith and who we are in Christ as born again believers. Through men like Oral Roberts the Holy Spirit gave revelation that God is good and He wants to do good for His people. God began to shower blessings upon His people and the prosperity movement was born.

However, Satan created subtle devices to counter this Christian movement. He sowed tares within the wheat—those who claimed to be Christian, but never really knew Christ. Some pursued Christianity only for monetary gain. A watered down gospel began to emerge; one void of Christ's demanding truths. Many in the church spent their energy trying to amass material wealth. Huge crowds began to attend conferences on prosperity and positive thinking.

No one dared speak of repentance, holiness, sacrifice, servanthood, or judgment. Though taught in the Bible, these subjects became taboo in American culture. So it became popular for one to say he was a Christian, but unpopular to actually live it.

Although God began the prosperity movement primarily for His persecuted people in Eastern Europe and poor third world nations, it was twisted by Satan. After the Iron Curtain fell toward the end of the 20th century, God was ready to lead the church in a new direction. However, many weren't willing to leave the prosperity movement. Some took the truth from this movement to an extreme.

While focusing on enjoying God's prosperity we all but forgot about the poor and the hurting. While enjoying our new affluence, we seemed to lose sight of those who had never heard the gospel, those held captive to sin. Rather than believing for lost souls to come home to the Father, we were appropriating our faith for huge houses and luxury cars; only things which benefited us personally.

As a result, many attained a mental assent that Jesus was God's Son. However, they never made Him Lord. They wanted Christ in their lives to give them what they wanted, to satisfy their fleshly appetites. But Jesus isn't a Santa Claus. Jesus took our judgment upon Himself. He offers us a way of escape from sin's judgment. But in return, He demands surrender to His will. He expects to see the fruit of sincere repentance. Many today refuse to repent because they love darkness rather than light (John 3:19).

Those who truly desire to obey Christ are persecuted as being intolerant, fanatics, and legalists. Today, those who preach repentance, justice, and holiness are labeled negative, doomsday preachers, even though they may preach with compassion. In some countries in Western Europe, those who stand against the vices of today are even arrested as hate mongers. In America, Christians have their lives threatened for standing up for the truth. Those who demand tolerance for their sinful lifestyle are very intolerant of Christians who truly practice their beliefs, even threatening their very lives.

Elijah faced similar persecution. Not only was he ridiculed by many in Israel, but his life was threatened. After putting so many of Baal's prophets to death, Elijah had become spent from all the bloodshed. He also grew tired from the constant persecution. He became so weary of the daily buffeting by the godless, he finally asked God to take his life.

God understands our human frailties and is touched by our human weaknesses (Hebrews 4:15). Notice God didn't chastise Elijah for lack of faith. God knew Elijah had grown weary from the spiritual warfare. Instead, God encouraged him, sending an angel to minister to Elijah. God was so pleased with Elijah He decided to take him from this earth to be with Him in heaven, just as He took Enoch hundreds of years before.

God began to make preparations for Elijah to leave the earth. God instructed Elijah to anoint Elisha, Jehu, and Hazael to finish the job. God would use Hazael, Jehu, and Elisha to finish judgment upon Israel. God told Elijah to anoint Hazael as king over Aram. Hazael put to death many in Israel who refused to repent and lay down their idols. Then Jehu, who was anointed as Israel's next king, killed whoever escaped Hazael. Elisha, Elijah's successor, destroyed all who escaped Jehu.

So Elijah went to find his successor, Elisha. He found Elisha plowing with oxen on his parents' farm. Elisha was an ordinary farmer who served the extraordinary God of the universe. Note God didn't call a prince, noble, or great military leader to replace Elijah. He didn't call a doctor or lawyer. He didn't call the respected Pharisee, priest, or religious leader of the day. Nor did he call the educated, but an ordinary farmer who dared to believe; an ordinary farmer who was busy doing his daily chores. God will always call the ordinary to do the extraordinary.

Elijah threw his cloak around Elisha. Elisha was well aware of what this meant. The cloak represented Elijah's anointing. Elisha knew God had chosen him to walk in Elijah's anointing. Elisha left everything to follow God. He told his parents goodbye, killed his oxen, and offered them as a sacrifice unto God. I believe Elisha killed his oxen to burn the bridges of his past. The most precious thing, his livelihood, he sacrificed to God. There was no going back to farming. He no longer had oxen to plow. The most precious people in his life, he kissed goodbye. He abandoned himself to the call, just as Jesus' Apostles did hundreds of years later.

He set out to follow Elijah and became his servant. He received intense training in the anointing. Elijah knew there was little time remaining. Soon he was to leave this life. So he gave Elisha a crash course on the prophet's office. He personally taught and mentored Elisha, who later became his successor as the leading prophet of Israel.

Confronting Kings

Elijah's time on earth was drawing to a close. But first, God had more business which needed Elijah's immediate attention.

Then the word of the LORD came to Elijah the Tishbite: "Go down to meet Ahab king of Israel, who rules in Samaria. He is now in Naboth's vineyard, where he has gone to take possession of it."

—1 Kings 21:17-18

God had shown amazing grace and forgiveness toward Ahab and his household. After Baal's prophets were destroyed, God sent rain on the kingdom of Israel, signifying forgiveness toward King Ahab and Israel. But Ahab seemed to be ungrateful, failing to appreciate God's bountiful mercies.

Ahab began to covet his neighbor's vineyard. Naboth's vineyard was close to King Ahab's palace. He said to Naboth, "Let me have your vineyard to use as a vegetable garden since it's close to my palace. I will give you a better vineyard, or if you prefer, I will pay you whatever you think it's worth."

But Naboth replied, "God forbid I should give you the inheritance of my fathers."

Ahab's request seemed fair. However, keep in mind the Jews placed great importance on ancestral linage. To Naboth, it wasn't just a vineyard, but his fathers' vineyard, handed down through the generations. It contained great sentimental, emotional, and traditional significance for Naboth. God's Law given through Moses encouraged the Israelites to keep land in the same tribe and family through the generations.

When Naboth rejected Ahab's offer, Ahab went home angry. He laid on his bed pouting and refused to eat. His wife Jezebel came in asking, "Why are you so sullen? Why won't you eat?"

He bemoaned his sad story to Jezebel like a child pouting for a toy.

Jezebel consoled her husband, "Is this how you act as king over Israel? Cheer up and eat. I'll get you the vineyard."

Jezebel wrote letters to the nobles who lived in Naboth's city with him. The letters instructed them to arrest Naboth on false charges and have him stoned. They hired witnesses to testify falsely against him saying he had cursed both God and king. So they took him outside the city and stoned him to death. The cry of Naboth's blood went up unto God.

Some who use their power to do wickedness may think they will escape. Some in powerful places believe they are above justice. They rule with fear and intimidation. But the God of heaven knows and sees. He delights in justice and mercy.

When Ahab heard Naboth was dead, he went and took possession of his vineyard. Immediately God instructed Elijah to go meet Ahab in Naboth's vineyard. God still referred to the vineyard as belonging to Naboth, even though he was dead and Ahab had taken possession of it.

When Ahab looked up and saw Elijah coming toward him, dread overtook him. He realized he and his wife Jezebel had done a terrible thing. God had given him the chance to repent, bringing rain and restoring life to his kingdom, but King Ahab continued in his evil ways. God instructed Elijah,

> Say to him, "This is what the LORD says: 'Have you not murdered a man and seized his property?'" Then say to him, "This is what the LORD says: 'In the place where dogs licked up Naboth's blood, dogs will lick up your blood—yes, yours!'"
>
> —1 Kings 21:19

Ahab exclaimed, "So you have found me, my enemy!" Because Elijah confronted him over evil, pronouncing judgment at God's instructions, he considered Elijah as his enemy. Today, when preachers of righteousness confront the evils of society, the godless consider them as enemies. For instance, those bound by sexual perversion consider Christians as their enemy because we confront their lifestyle. On the contrary, we aren't their enemies, but their friends. Who else loves them enough to confront them with truth that will set them free?

> Wounds from a friend can be trusted, but an enemy multiplies kisses.
>
> —Proverbs 27:6

Love constrains us to warn them this lifestyle only leads to death. God desires they come out of bondage into a life of joy and peace. God's love motivates us to rescue them from their destructive lifestyle.

Love, as well as justice, motivated God to confront Ahab and hold him accountable through the prophet Elijah. But Ahab's rebellion blinded him to God's love. He saw Elijah only as an enemy who disrupted his life of pleasure; an enemy who was always faultfinding; one that was out to destroy his kingdom.

Throughout his reign Ahab worshipped other Gods. He failed to heed the advice of Elijah, but consulted with ungodly council. Eventually Ahab was killed in battle when Hazael led the Aremeans against Israel. Elijah's prophecy came to pass and the dogs licked up Ahab's blood in the same place where Naboth was stoned.

His son Ahaziah began to reign after Ahab's death. Ahaziah continued to worship Baal just as his father Ahab. Like Ahab he consulted with Baal's prophets rather than God's prophets. He esteemed other gods and their prophets over the one true God. Just like his father Ahab, Ahaziah saw Elijah as an enemy rather than a friend. Elijah confronted the king and the people with the truth. He was unafraid of the king or what the people thought. Elijah would often prophesy judgment upon the king and the nation. So Ahaziah viewed Elijah with fear and disdain trying to avoid him. He preferred consulting Baal's prophets rather than God's.

One day King Ahaziah fell through the lattice in the upper room of his house in Samaria and injured himself. He sent messengers to consult Baal-Zebub the God of Ekron to see if he'd recover from his injury. The Lord's angel said to Elijah, "Go up and meet the king of Samaria's messengers and ask them, 'Is it because there is no God in Israel you are going off to consult Baal-Zebub, the god of Ekron?' Therefore this is what the LORD says: 'You will not leave the bed you are lying on. You will certainly die!'" Elijah went and obeyed.

The messengers shortly returned to Ahaziah. Ahaziah realizing they couldn't have possibly made the trip to Ekron in such a short time asked the messengers, "Why have you come back?"

Unable to recognize Elijah, the messengers told Ahaziah what Elijah had said. The king asked, "What kind of man was it who told you this?"

They replied, "He was a man with fur clothes and a leather belt around his waist." Immediately the king knew from the description it was Elijah.

The king sent a captain of his army with fifty men to bring back Elijah. The captain approached Elijah who was sitting at the top of the hill. "Man of God, the king says come down," the captain commanded.

Perhaps Elijah was afraid of what the king might do to him. Perhaps the captain acted disrespectfully. Maybe Elijah wanted the king to know that because of his rebellion by worshipping other gods and consulting them rather than the true God, Ahaziah had no authority over him. Elijah was careful to follow God's instructions closely. So it's conceivable he was simply obeying God when Elijah answered the captain, "If I am a man of God, may fire come down from heaven and consume you and your fifty men!" In a great demonstration of power and authority, fire immediately fell from heaven and consumed the captain and his men.

When the king heard of it he sent another captain with fifty men. The captain approached Elijah and forcefully commanded him, "Man of God, this is what the king says, 'Come down at once!'"

Again, Elijah replied, "If I am a man of God, may fire come down from heaven and consume you and your fifty men." At Elijah's word, fire came down from heaven and destroyed those men also. Elijah remembered Jezebel's vow to have him killed. Could it be that he suspected Ahaziah may be angry with him for prophesying that he wouldn't recover from his accident? Elijah wasn't about to let these men lead him to his death. He knew the powerful anointing upon his life. He had the faith to believe whatever he spoke would come to pass. Elijah realized God esteemed the prophet's office as much as kings. God's authority was higher than man's.

I believe Rev. Billy Graham has had this authority from God. From Eisenhower to Clinton, Billy Graham acted as spiritual advisor to leaders of the most powerful nation on earth. For many years he was voted as the most admired person in the United States, even above the president. At one point some tried to persuade him to run for president of the United States. Mr. Graham responded by saying he refused to lower his calling to become president. He knew God's high calling in Christ which was upon his life. He realized the authority of his office given to him by the King of kings.

Billy Graham was God's ambassador, God's spokesperson. He spoke to many kings, prime ministers, and presidents across the earth. He carried with him great influence and authority. How did he gain this influence and authority? As he demonstrated Christ's character, he grew in favor with God and with man. By faith Billy Graham pleased

God. Although he packs tremendous authority, he was and remains a very humble man.

Likewise, the Pope, if truly called by God and submitted to the Holy Spirit carries authority just as kings and presidents. Ideally, the Pope is appointed by God through holy men led by God's Spirit. If he walks in humility and obeys God's Word, he will have favor with God and with man.

The king, who had just heard his death sentence from the prophet Elijah, wasn't to be deterred. He sent a third captain with fifty men. Unlike the previous captains, this captain didn't address Elijah with disrespect. He didn't rudely demand Elijah to come with him. This captain approached Elijah and fell on his knees in humility. Having heard what happened to the previous captains, he reverenced Elijah and his God with holy fear. "Man of God," he begged, "Please have respect for my life and the lives of these fifty men, your servants! See, fire has fallen from heaven and consumed the first two captains and all their men. But now have respect for my life!"

Elijah may have well called down fire from heaven again, but the Lord's angel spoke to him, "Go down with him. Do not be afraid of him." So Elijah went with the captain. Upon arriving, he told King Ahaziah face to face the same message he had given to the king's messengers. So Ahaziah died according to the Word the Lord had spoken through Elijah.

The Departure

Elijah knew his time on earth was drawing to a close. God was satisfied with the work he had done. He obeyed God fully with his whole heart. By faith Elijah had confronted the people of Israel with their idols. He destroyed Baal's prophets and set Israel on a course for revival. He taught and mentored other prophets.

But his great victories weren't without a price. From early childhood Satan had buffeted Elijah, knowing God's hand was upon him. Having boldly confronted popular opinion, he endured much persecution and hardship. He chose to remain single, forsaking comforts; the blessing of a good wife and family, for the sake of God's call upon his life. Battle weary, Elijah was ready to leave this world and enter into God's rest. God had prepared a magnificent departure and homecoming for Elijah.

News quickly spread among the prophets that God was about to take Elijah home. I believe the prophets sensed in their spirits, that day was the day Elijah would depart. The way in which Elijah departed may foreshadow the Church's rapture. I believe the day Jesus comes for His bride, those who are looking for his coming will know, just as the prophets of Israel knew when the time had arrived for Elijah's departure. We won't know the hour or the date until the day arrives (Matthew 24:36). But those who are watching and waiting won't be caught completely by surprise. Jesus said we can know the season (Matthew 24:32-33). Just as the prophets anticipated the day had arrived for Elijah to depart, those who are walking in the Spirit on the Day of the Lord will begin to anticipate something is about to happen. The Messiah's coming will take the world by surprise, but those whose lamps are filled with oil will be ready (Matthew 25:1-13). Jesus also said, "Wherever there is a carcass, there the eagles will gather" (Matthew 24:28).

Everywhere Elijah and Elisha went, the prophets approached Elisha. "Do you know the Lord is going to take your master from you today?" they quizzed. Elijah struck the Jordan River with his cloak and the waters parted. He tried to persuade Elisha to remain as he continued into the wilderness across the Jordan River. But Elisha wouldn't be dissuaded. I believe the same faith, the same persistence will be in those who go up in the rapture. They will rise above the worldly cares to pursue fellowship with God. When the world tries to persuade and pressure these radical Christians to conform, they'll refuse to turn back from following Christ just as Elisha refused to turn back from following Elijah.

Elisha recognized he was about to replace Elijah and finish the work of leading Israel back to God. He realized he would need the same power that was upon Elijah. He was determined to receive Elijah's anointing. As Elijah crossed the Jordan River on dry ground, his student followed close behind.

After they had crossed the Jordan, Elijah turned to Elisha and asked, "Tell me, is there anything I can do for you before I am taken?" In the true spirit of servanthood, Elijah was still looking to bless others. He wanted to impart one final blessing on his student who had faithfully served him with respect and honor.

"Let me inherit a double portion of your spirit," Elisha replied.

"You have asked a difficult thing," Elijah said, "yet if you see me when I am taken from you, it will be yours."

They continued walking in the wilderness, talking together. They enjoyed what they knew would be their final moments together. Perhaps they spoke of the work still to be done in Israel. Perhaps they spoke of the future; what God's Spirit was revealing to them. As the sky began to darken and the wind to blow, both could sense God's tangible presence. It was a holy moment; one Elisha would remember the rest of his days. The wind intensified and they could hear a rumbling sound as that of thunder. As they neared the place of Elijah's departure, they remained silent with holy reverence and anticipation. They could now sense God's awesome presence. As they walked together, suddenly a chariot and horses of fire appeared and separated the two of them, and Elijah went up to heaven in a whirlwind. Just as his predecessor Enoch, Elijah walked with God and he was not, for God took him.

The divine visitation so startled Elisha he cried out, "My father! My father! The chariots and the horsemen of Israel!"

I believe these were warring angels assigned to guard and protect Israel. In reverential fear, Elisha tore his clothes. The skies began to clear, the wind to subside. The sun appeared again and all was silent. As Elisha regained his composure, there lying on the ground was the cloak of Elijah which fell from the sky. With holy reverence and gratefulness he picked up the cloak and walked back toward the Jordan River. As he put on Elijah's cloak, God's Spirit of faith began to rise up within Elisha, the same Spirit of faith that was in Elijah. He took the cloak, struck the water with it and cried out, "Where now is the Lord, the God of Elijah?" When he struck the water, it divided, and he crossed over on dry ground. The spirit of Elijah had come upon him. He'd continue the work Elijah had begun.

Elijah set a precedent and paved the way for prophets who followed him. The Bible implies he taught at a school of prophets. His boldness and faith set a high standard for other prophets to follow. He taught and trained Elisha, who later became his successor as Israel's leading prophet.

In the same way, God is raising up men and women like Elijah who will boldly proclaim the truth. They will bring the nations to the valley of decision, preaching justice, truth, righteousness, and mercy. Signs and wonders will follow the preaching of God's righteousness. Elijah was a preacher of righteousness. Despite his human frailties, God used Elijah to bring a great revival to Israel.

Like Noah, Elijah's faith, obedience and his stand for righteousness condemned the rest of Israel. Elijah walked with God. He knew God's heart. God loved Elijah and spent much time with him. Elijah didn't see death, but ascended into heaven in grand style. Many from the school of prophets witnessed the awesome sight. Elijah walked with God and was not, for God took him.

Chapter 5

A VOICE
IN THE WILDERNESS

IT WAS TWILIGHT in Jerusalem. The sunset glistened on the temple walls. Zechariah trekked toward the temple to administer his priestly duties. He was dressed in priestly garments; the tunic, the robe of the ephod, the ephod itself and the breast piece. The ephod was fastened on him by the skillfully woven waistband. On his head was the turban with the attached sacred diadem. Anointing oil was poured on Zechariah's head. Before he could minister the sacrifice offerings for the people, a sin offering had to be made for Zechariah. The Priests had very detailed and tedious instructions.

It was time for the yearly atonement on the altar of incense. Once a year, the priest was to make atonement on the horns of the altar. The annual atonement was made with the blood from the atoning sin offering. No other incense could be burned on this altar. No other burnt offering, grain offering, or drink offering could be made. This altar was reserved strictly for the blood from the atoning sin offering. God had told Moses this offering was most holy to the Lord. This atonement represented Christ laying Himself on the altar as a sin offering for all of mankind. Therefore, it was very holy to the Lord.

Zechariah approached the altar to place fresh incense there. The incense burned, filling the air with a wonderful fragrance. The incense was to burn regularly before the Lord as God had instructed Moses many generations before.

He and his wife, Elizabeth, loved the Lord with a heart for God's commandments. He had always been faithful in his priestly duties. He served God faithfully and ministered to the people. Zechariah and his wife showed compassion to the poor and needy.

Zechariah and Elizabeth had always wanted a son. But his wife had been unable to conceive. He and Elizabeth had knelt before God and asked for a son, but years passed and nothing happened. Now growing old in years, he had given up any hope of having a child. He resolved to be content in carrying out his priestly duties. There must be a good reason why God didn't answer his prayer. Zechariah knew God could be trusted. He decided not to look back in regret, but to continue serving God with joy.

With incense burning, Zechariah poured oil into the lamps. As he tended to the lamps, the people waited outside praying with an attitude of repentance and reverence. This was a holy moment when atonement was offered to God for the people's sins. He felt grateful to serve a forgiving, merciful God. As he worked at the altar of incense, he sensed God's presence. With awe and reverence, Zechariah began to light the lamps.

> Then an angel of the Lord appeared to him, standing at the right side of the altar of incense. When Zechariah saw him, he was startled and was gripped with fear. But the angel said to him: "Do not be afraid, Zechariah; your prayer has been heard. Your wife Elizabeth will bear you a son, and you are to give him the name John. He will be a joy and delight to you, and many will rejoice because of his birth, for he will be great in the sight of the Lord. He is never to take wine or other fermented drink, and he will be filled with the Holy Spirit even from birth. Many of the people of Israel will he bring back to the Lord their God. And he will go on before the Lord, in the spirit and power of Elijah, to turn the hearts of the fathers to their children and the disobedient to the wisdom of the righteous—to make ready a people prepared for the Lord."
>
> —Luke 1:11-17

The angel told him the baby would be filled with the Holy Spirit from the time he is born. His son would bring many people back to God.

Zechariah began to question of such a seemingly impossible occurrence and asked the angel, "How can I be sure of this? For I am an old man, and my wife is well along in years."

The angel assured Zechariah of his identity and authority, "I am Gabriel, who stands in God's presence, and I was sent to speak to you and tell you this good news."

Gabriel declared he was one who stood in God's presence. What greater authority than to stand in God's presence? Yet we as believers have God's presence within us. Gabriel went on to say Zechariah would be unable to speak because he didn't believe his words (Luke 1:19-20). This visitation occurred at the hour of incense when the whole assembly of people was praying outside. Now the people who were outside praying began to wonder why Zechariah stayed so long in the sanctuary. When he finally came out, he couldn't speak to them. Being somewhat familiar with the spiritual realm, the people realized he had seen a vision. He kept making signs to them, but couldn't speak. The people were astonished.

The child's name was to be John. He would be a preacher of righteousness. As in the past, Satan tried to prevent one of God's preachers from fulfilling his destiny by making Elizabeth, John's mother, barren for many years. Once again, God proved His faithfulness by overcoming the devil's schemes. She conceived baby John in her later years. He was born about six months before the Christ. John had a very unique birth.

Shortly after, Elizabeth conceived as the angel foretold. When John was still in his mother's womb, Mary, the mother of Jesus came to visit them. At the sound of Mary's voice both John and his mother were filled with the Holy Spirit and he leaped in his mother's womb (Luke 1:41). As a result, John was aware of God's presence even as a child.

Upon hearing the good news of John's birth, Elizabeth's neighbors and friends rejoiced with her. Although Elizabeth was advanced in years, God had shown this barren woman mercy by blessing her with a son. How wonderful! They went with them to circumcise the child on the eighth day as was the Jewish custom. The priests, friends, and relatives expected her to name the child Zechariah, after his father. Instead, Elizabeth insisted, "His name will be called John."

Surprised, they replied to Elizabeth, "None of your relatives have the name John." Still not convinced, they turned to look at Zechariah. He asked for a writing tablet and wrote, "His name is John." Immediately his tongue was loosed and he began to praise God. Then, Zechariah was filled with the Holy Spirit and began to prophesy:

> Praise be to the Lord, the God of Israel, because He has come and has redeemed His people. He has raised up a horn of salvation for us in the house of his servant David ... to rescue us from the hand of our enemies, and to enable us to serve him without fear in holiness and righteousness before him all our days. And you, my child, will be called a prophet of the Most High; for you will go on before the Lord to prepare the way for him, to give his people the knowledge of salvation through the forgiveness of their sins.
> —Luke 1:68-69; 74-77

The people were all amazed and the fear of God came upon them. The scriptures say this event was talked about throughout the hill country of Judea. Many people took note of this unusual phenomenon and wondered about the destiny of this child.

Preparing for Destiny

Like his forerunner, Elijah, God prepared John for his destiny. Since Elizabeth was barren for so many years, John's parents were older when he was born. Because young couples had children at a very young age in ancient times, Elizabeth and Zechariah were likely old enough to be his grandparents. By the time John was a young man, it's probable both his parents were no longer alive. An only child, he was left alone with no immediate family. Indeed, many of those who witnessed his miraculous birth were old or no longer living. Since so many marveled at the unusual circumstances of his birth, one would think his parents may have sent him to a theological school of his day, or one of the prestigious Pharisees would take him under his wings for training. At least, he could follow in the footsteps of his father, performing his priestly duties. Being advanced in years, perhaps his parents passed away before they could find someone to train him. John's free spirit may have left him disappointed at the prospect of memorizing all the details of the priestly duties. He would have felt trapped and confined by the priest's everyday rituals. But thirty years later, we find him, not among the learned, not among the religious leaders, not among the priests, but living alone in the wilderness. It's possible he lived many years in the wilderness depending on the timing of his parents' death.

I perceive John as a man's man; a great outdoorsman; rugged as was Elijah. He was uncomfortable in the city. He didn't like the hustle and bustle of the busy streets in Jerusalem, but the gentle sound of the Jordan River, as it flowed toward the Dead Sea. He avoided crowds for the open space of the Judean wilderness. He shunned his father's priestly duties and embraced the freedom of the wild. To John, the temple's priestly duties were too confining, the learned schools, too rigid. Besides, God didn't want John to learn the scribes and Pharisees' erroneous traditions. Having become wise in their own eyes, some of the religious leaders hadn't a clue concerning the spirit of the Law. They misinterpreted God's meaning and the Law's intent. Some rabbis through the years added unnecessary burdens and man's traditions.

John was prepared for his ministry in the Holy Spirit's school. He learned to hear God's voice at an early age. He wasn't trained by the Pharisees or religious educators. He learned by studying the scriptures, while living in the wilderness. Why waste time learning men's doctrines when you have God, Himself, as the teacher?

To the Scribes and Pharisees, John was an unlikely candidate to be the Messiah's forerunner. He was uneducated in the schools of Judaism. He wasn't considered a traditional religious leader. To the religious leaders, John was an outsider claiming God gave him authority to preach. He had no training, no oratorical skills. He didn't observe men's traditions which were added to the Law, from which the Pharisees measured greatness. They arrogantly viewed John with contempt and disdain. He had shunned his duties as priest for a peculiar life of seclusion in the wilderness.

Having spent his time in the wilderness, he was relatively unknown to the people before he began his ministry. Until God made public the ministry of John, few knew of his existence. Notwithstanding, the angel told Zechariah, "Your son will be great in God's sight." Although no one else knew about John the Baptist, God knew him well.

John was a Nazirite. He was consecrated unto God. A razor never cut his hair. He avoided drinking wine. He was made holy, set apart unto the Lord. Since he lived in the wilderness, he was shielded from the world's corruption and from the laws and traditions of men. He fed his mind and heart with God's pure inspired Word. For this reason, John could preach with boldness and confidence. With little distractions in the isolated Judean wilderness, he learned to hear God's voice.

The Baptist knew God had a special destiny for him. I can almost see him as he walked through the Judean wilderness, the wind blowing his long hair and beard. I see him looking for locusts and wild honey, his skin dry, his face tanned and parched from the sun. He had the pleasant smell of leather and the wild. He lived with a sense of destiny.

The Baptist's preaching was blunt and to the point. He evidently meditated on the Holy Scriptures, because you find him quoting them often. During his time in the wilderness, the Holy Spirit showed John things to come. God's kingdom was at hand and John was to prepare the way. I believe John knew he was called to prepare the way of the Lord, long before he gained public notoriety. However, it took some time for God to prepare him.

John sensed God's hand upon his life. He thought of Abraham and the prophets of the past. He was walking in the very same paths they had walked; the old ancient paths of truth (Jeremiah 6:16). The same Spirit, which rested upon these holy men, was upon him. He felt a special kinship with Elijah. He had read and studied much about Elijah. It was almost as if he knew him. As John continued to meditate on the scriptures, he began to see the brevity of this life on earth compared to eternity. What was his purpose? How did he fit into God's plan? As he looked at the stars on a cool desert evening, perhaps he contemplated what lay ahead. When God calls His preachers of righteousness, He often gives them a glimpse, sometimes even visions of what's to come. I believe John had an inward witness of his divine purpose.

Although he wasn't quite sure who the Messiah was, John had revelation the Messiah was about to reveal Himself soon. John was called to tear down all things that hindered the people from hearing the Messiah; to soften the hard hearts leading the people to humility and repentance. Only by making the crooked paths straight could the people of Israel recognize their hour of visitation. Only by bringing the mountains and hills low, could the leaders see the need for a Messiah. John would bring low the wealthy, famous, and prideful. The prophet would fill the valleys, allowing the common and poor to realize how valuable they were in God's sight. John was the first to preach that all men are created equal. He was called to make the rough ways of rebellion smooth. Only by a heartfelt repentance could God's people receive the Messiah's healing and restoration.

As time passed, John discovered the important mission he had; still here he was in the wilderness. No one knew of his existence, much less the significant purpose for which he had been called.

With this revelation burning in his innermost being, John likely wondered when his chance would come. He may have had many questions. How long will be the time of preparation? Why did God give him such revelation? Did God anoint him just to live a secluded life? Surely the truths revealed concerning the Messiah weren't buried with John in the wilderness. As he drank from the Jordan River's pure water, he contemplated when his time would come to preach to the nation of Israel.

> And the child grew and became strong in spirit; and he lived in the desert until he appeared publicly to Israel.
>
> —Luke 1:80

The angel declared John would turn the fathers' hearts to the children and the disobedient to God's wisdom. John would humble men as children and teach the disobedient God's truth. God had to plant His thoughts in John, to work on his heart. He made John bold and fearless.

He spent years learning the scriptures. We find him quoting them often. His seclusion in the wilderness was for a season.

The Day Arrives

Finally, after years of preparation, John's season arrived. Suddenly, he burst upon the scene. John began to make disciples, teaching them from the Law and the prophets. His disciples fasted and prayed often (Luke 5:33, Matthew 9:14, Mark 2:18).

As word of this fiery prophet spread, crowds began to come from all over Israel and gather around him to hear his message from God.

> He went into all the country around the Jordan, preaching a baptism of repentance for the forgiveness of sins. As is written in the book of the words of Isaiah the prophet: "A voice of one calling in the desert, 'Prepare the way for the Lord, make straight paths for him. Every valley shall be filled in, every mountain and hill made low. The crooked roads shall become straight, the rough ways smooth. And all mankind will see God's salvation.'"
>
> —Luke 3:3-6

John came onto the scene preaching repentance. One of my favorite classes in college was the Consumer Behavior class in the Marketing department. There was one principal of marketing I've never forgotten. In general, people are resistant to change. The natural tendency of man is to stay in the comfort zone. Most of us have the mindset, "Don't rock my boat. Don't take any action that will inconvenience me or make me uncomfortable. Don't interrupt my pleasure."

Consumers seem frustrated with remodeling or changes in the order of a store's merchandise. They prefer to enter the store and know exactly where everything is. A large retail store changed the location and order of their merchandise once a year. They'd discontinue some of the old items and bring in some new ones. Every year, there was a barrage of complaints from the customers over the new changes.

Physiologists rated the high stress factors in a person's life. Virtually all high stress levels had to do with change; relocating to a new job or new city; marriage; the loss of a loved one through death or divorce. Change requires us to leave our comfort zone. Even if the change for the long run results in tremendous improvements in our lifestyles, some will choose to remain in their present state and miss the wonderful opportunities awaiting them.

The same principal is true spiritually. To enter God's kingdom requires change. Let's surrender to God with childlike humility. We can change our way of thinking to have the mind of Christ. John the Baptist preached this message. Jesus preached this principal at the beginning of His ministry, "Jesus came … preaching the gospel of God's kingdom, and saying, 'the time is fulfilled, and God's kingdom is at hand: repent (change) and believe the gospel'" (Mark 1:14-15).

John wasn't afraid of others' opinions. His purpose was to prepare the way of the Lord, not to make people feel good. John was called not to comfort, but to make people uncomfortable with the sword of God's Word. Unlike Jesus, John did no miracles, but the miracle of bringing people to repentance.

The Baptist's methods were strange to the religious leaders of his day. He didn't teach in the synagogue, as was the custom for the rabbi. He didn't consult with the high priest or other teachers. He didn't try to promote his ministry. He didn't go to the cities trying to gain an audience. But he remained in the wilderness and God promoted John's work. News soon traveled about his prophetic ministry and the crowds were flocking to see him. The Baptist taught with authority, mentioning the Messiah's soon coming, as if he were totally assured His words would come to pass. He preached as though he had personally conversed with God Himself. He baptized the converts in the river Jordan as a symbol of repentance and remission of sin.

He didn't preach a message of prosperity. He never asked for donations, but found his sustenance from the wilderness. He was anointed with the Spirit of Elijah. Those who preach truth may not receive huge donations. If John were preaching today, he'd probably be labeled as a hellfire and brimstone preacher. Some would accuse him of being negative; judgmental. The press would call him a right wing religious fanatic. He may be misunderstood as a troublemaker, with little love for people. On the contrary, it was for love John preached his strong message of repentance.

> See, I will make you into a threshing sledge, new and sharp, with many teeth. You will thresh the mountains and crush them, and reduce the hills to chaff.
>
> —Isaiah 41:15

> See, today I appoint you over nations and kingdoms to uproot and tear down, to destroy and overthrow, to build and to plant.
>
> —Jeremiah 1:10

God used John to expose the sins of men. The preaching of John demanded change. Like other preachers of righteousness, John warned of coming judgment for those who refuse to repent. John the Baptist didn't have connections with the rich and famous. He didn't take a course on leadership, positive thinking, or how to win and influence people. Nor did he try to get a position at the local synagogue. John the Baptist didn't have a program for the poor or a Bible school. He wasn't called to start such programs. The Baptist didn't have a charismatic personality. He just began preaching in the wilderness and the people came. John didn't take it upon himself to become a great preacher. He was called by God from his mother's womb. The people of Israel recognized his anointing and came from every walk of life to hear John.

> John said to the crowds coming out to be baptized by him, "You brood of vipers! Who warned you to flee from the coming wrath? Produce fruit in keeping with repentance. And do not begin to say to yourselves, 'We have Abraham as our father.' For I tell you that out of these stones God can raise up children for Abraham. The ax is already at the root of the trees, and every tree that does not produce good fruit will be cut down and thrown into the fire."
> —Luke 3:7-9

Some prideful ones, and those who didn't like the idea of repentance, began to make excuses. The Baptist warned the people against making excuses, "Do not begin to say to yourselves, 'We have Abraham as our father.'" Some didn't receive his message. Some felt that since they were Jews and tried to obey the Law, they had no need to repent.

"We know God's Word just as you do. Why do you act as though we are evil? We are in covenant with God. We have Abraham as our father," they argued.

What similar words ring in the church today. Some in the church make excuses when confronted with sin, "Don't tell us we need to change. God loves us the way we are. We'll have none of this condemnation. We're not under the Law, but under grace."

The words of John cut into the people's hearts. He brought the fear of the Lord to the people of Israel who believed his message. John the

Baptist prepared the way by tearing down the idols in people's lives. At his preaching, the Holy Spirit searched the hearts of God's people and rooted out the weeds in their hearts. He was sent to burn out the wood, hay, and stubble so only the gold and silver remained. John plowed up the hard, stony ground of their hearts. Therefore, when Jesus appeared on the scene, many people were ready to receive him. Those who had repented of their sins were ready to receive the love of Christ. Those who were cleaned by God's Word could have the faith to believe and receive the miracles of Jesus.

But not all received John's message.

> But when he saw many of the Pharisees and Sadducees coming to where he was baptizing, he said to them: "You brood of vipers! Who warned you to flee from the coming wrath?
>
> —Matthew 3:7

Those who rejected John's message of repentance also rejected Jesus as the Messiah. Some of the Pharisees, Sadducees, and leaders were envious and questioned John's authority. Just like everyone else, they failed to meet God's requirements of perfection. They were too prideful to admit their need for change. But many of the common people repented at the preaching of John.

> "What should we do then?" the crowd asked. John answered, "The man with two tunics should share with him who has none, and the one who has food should do the same." Tax collectors also came to be baptized. "Teacher," they asked, "what should we do?" "Don't collect any more than you are required to," he told them.
>
> Then some soldiers asked him, "And what should we do?"
>
> He replied, "Don't extort money and don't accuse people falsely— be content with your pay." The people were waiting expectantly and were all wondering in their hearts if John might possibly be the Christ.
>
> —Luke 3:10-15

John preached with the spirit of Elijah and it stirred people to change. They began to ask John what to do. Notice how specific John was in his answers. He gave examples on how to be generous. He told the publicans not to be dishonest or greedy. To the Roman soldiers he replied, "Do not commit unnecessary violence, neither accuse falsely." He also admonished them to be content with what they had. John knew discontentment could lead to sin.

What was the result of John preaching righteousness? The people were in great expectation. When we repent and get right with God, we begin to expect great things from God. Then God can move in mighty, miraculous ways. On the contrary, if we take offence to this type of preaching, and persist in evil ways, we'll perish as in the days of Noah. Many responded to John's preaching. Because they heeded John's warnings, they were ready to receive Jesus, the Messiah. By the time Jesus came on the scene, there was great expectation.

> John answered them all, "I baptize you with water. But one more powerful than I will come, the thongs of whose sandals I am not worthy to untie. He will baptize you with the Holy Spirit and with fire. His winnowing fork is in his hand to clear his threshing floor and to gather the wheat into his barn, but he will burn up the chaff with unquenchable fire."
>
> —Luke 3:16-17

Finishing the Race

John was always pointing toward Jesus and giving God the glory. One called of God must beware of magnifying himself. A true minister of God will always magnify Christ.

> They came to John and said to him, Rabbi, that man who was with you on the other side of the Jordan—the one you testified about—well, he is baptizing, and everyone is going to him. To this John replied, "A man can receive only what is given him from heaven. You yourselves can testify that I said, 'I am not the Christ but am sent ahead of him.' The bride belongs to the bridegroom. The friend who attends the bridegroom waits and listens for him, and is full of joy when he hears the bridegroom's voice. That joy is mine, and it is now complete. He must become greater; I must become less.
>
> —John 3:26-30

John stayed true to his calling, even when many began to leave his ministry and follow Christ. John wasn't envious of Jesus, but rejoiced to hear Him. John was thrilled at Jesus' success. John was confident of what God called him to do. However he didn't think of himself more highly than he should. When John's disciples questioned him concerning the crowd's shifting to Jesus, he humbly replied, "He must increase and I must decrease."

John wasn't concerned about popularity or big crowds, but doing God's will. If God were to draw all the crowds away to Jesus until no one was left, John wouldn't be disturbed. He'd go back to his life of communing with God in the seclusion of the wilderness. Besides, he wasn't very fond of huge crowds. His public ministry had been quite demanding. For the past year, he had little privacy, sometimes ministering to the crowds until he was on the brink of exhaustion. At such times, John felt he couldn't go much longer. As he turned to God for strength, he felt a surge of power.

Now and then, he longed for the days of silence when only the occasional desert wind's whisper could be heard; the only sound was birds making melody to their creator; or the Jordan River's trickling water. John could be perfectly content going back to his carefree life in the wilderness. From time to time, he could go hear Jesus teach, and return to the familiar confines of the wilderness. But alas, that wasn't to be. Like Jeremiah, God's Word was a burning fire within him and he couldn't be silent. He was compelled to complete his mission—to prepare the way.

John boldly confronted the leaders of his day, including King Herod. There is a misconception that the church shouldn't confront those in authority with the truth. Some say the church should stay out of politics and government. It's good to submit to laws of our authorities when it doesn't violate God's Word. In addition, we are to respect those who are in authority over us. Nevertheless this doesn't prohibit us from confronting corrupt leaders or disagreeing with their policies. We should make every effort to disagree peacefully and respectfully.

Now, Herod's brother, Philip, had a wife named Herodias. Herod had taken her to be his wife. John had been saying to Herod, "It is not lawful for you to have your brother's wife." For this reason, Herod had John thrown into prison.

So here was God's faithful prophet thrown into a dark dingy prison. I believe this was John's greatest test of faith as he sat confined in Herod's prison.

John could have reasoned, "Why did you allow this to happen, God? Have I not preached what you instructed me to? Have I not prepared the way for the Messiah?"

But John was a man of faith. John had received marvelous revelation while in the wilderness. However, there were still things to come which he didn't see clearly so far. He was convinced Jesus was the Messiah. John was confident Jesus would come and rescue him from this filthy prison. Like so many other Jews, John possibly saw Jesus as overthrowing Herod and the Roman government. Like Jesus' own disciples, John may have anticipated Jesus delivering the Jews from Roman occupation and physically restoring the kingdom of Israel. He saw Jesus as a mighty king reigning from Jerusalem in righteousness. He knew Herod, Pontius Pilate, and even the Roman emperor would one day bow to Jesus.

But as the days turned into weeks, and the weeks into months, John began to have his doubts. His free spirit was cramped by this confining prison. He missed the bright sun; the fresh scent of the outdoors; the peace of the Judean wilderness. Could his ministry be finished? He had much more truth to impart into God's people. Notwithstanding, here he was imprisoned like a caged animal. He anticipated his release so he might continue working for the kingdom. Perhaps he could assist with Jesus' ministry.

After months in prison with no relief in sight, John began to battle doubt. *This is not what I expected,* thought John. *I always heard God's voice so clearly. Perhaps in the pressure of public ministry, I missed God. Maybe Jesus is not the Messiah.* As hope of ever being released from prison began to fade, John continued to hear of Jesus' fame. He sent some of his disciples to Jesus to ask him, "Are you the one who was to come, or should we expect someone else?"

Jesus replied, "Go back and report to John what you hear and see: The blind receive sight, the lame walk, those who have leprosy are cured, the deaf hear, the dead are raised, and the good news is preached to the poor. Blessed is the man who does not fall away on account of me" (Matthew 11:2-6).

Although John didn't understand everything, he chose to trust God in faith. When John's disciples were recounting Jesus' words, John began to receive more understanding; *God's kingdom is not just an outward kingdom, but a kingdom that begins within the heart*. While it wasn't exactly as he expected, John had heard how Jesus was doing the works of God's kingdom.

As mentioned, John confronted Herod several times concerning his relationship with his brother's wife. As a result, Herodias nursed a grudge against John. From this time forth she looked for an opportunity to silence him. She wanted to kill him, but was unable to because Herod feared and respected John, knowing he was a righteous and holy man. Moreover, he was afraid of the people because they considered John a prophet.

On Herod's birthday Herodias threw a huge party for the king. She invited friends, dignitaries, and a host of wealthy people. That evening as Herod and his guests reveled, John felt uneasy in his spirit. He felt an evil presence. He could smell death. He feared for his life. But John knew what to do. He turned to God in prayer and God's presence filled the dark dungeon with a marvelous light. He began to hear God's voice in the inward man. His work on earth was done. Tonight was John's night of victory; his night of graduation. As John surrendered his will to God, his battle with fear ended. A peace swept over John as he resolved to accept his fate and lay down his life for God's kingdom. He would join the many other prophets who had laid down their lives for the truth.

Meanwhile at the celebration, the daughter of Herodias danced for them and pleased Herod so much, he promised with an oath to give her whatever she asked. The same lust that drove Herod into this adulterous relationship with his brother's wife enticed him to speak without wisdom. Prompted by her mother, she said, "Give me here on a platter the head of John the Baptist." The king was distressed, but because of the oaths he made before his dinner guests, he ordered her request to be granted.

As John heard the soldiers' footsteps, he knew his final hour had arrived. He had accomplished his mission; to restore the fathers' hearts to the children; to prepare the way of the Anointed One. He'd die with a clear conscience, knowing he had obeyed God. The soldiers were amazed at John's courage and calm composure as they tied his hands and forced him on his knees. The razor sharp glistening sword was raised above John's head. In an instant John's mission on this earth ended.

His head was brought in on a platter and given to the girl, who carried it to her mother. John's disciples came and took his body and buried it. Then they went and reported the tragic news to Jesus.

What Did You Go to the Wilderness to See?

John, the Baptist confronted King Herod and it cost him his life. It may cost us if we boldly take a stand for righteousness. Notwithstanding, we shall receive a crown of life and hear the words of our Master, "Well done, my good and faithful servant. Enter into your rest" (Matthew 25:20-23). Jesus commended John after hearing of his imprisonment:

> As John's disciples were leaving, Jesus began to speak to the crowd about John: "What did you go out into the desert to see? A reed swayed by the wind? If not, what did you go out to see? A man dressed in fine clothes? No, those who wear fine clothes are in kings' palaces. Then what did you go out to see? A prophet? Yes, I tell you, and more than a prophet. This is the one about whom it is written: 'I will send my messenger ahead of you, who will prepare your way before you.' I tell you the truth: Among those born of women there has not risen anyone greater than John the Baptist; yet he who is least in the kingdom of heaven is greater than he."
>
> —Matthew 11:7-11

The Baptist didn't have a charming personality. He wasn't the handsome Hollywood type. He wasn't trained in social etiquette. He didn't attend any religious school, nor was he a great leader or affiliated with great men of his day. He lacked the traditional qualifications of a well respected priest or Pharisee. The Baptist had no fancy titles or accreditations. He didn't have multiple degrees. He had no formal training in journalism, writing, public speaking or communication. He was relatively unknown before the day God catapulted him in to public fame. He didn't have any recommendations from famous or respected men, nor did the Baptist have years of experience in ministry. He didn't even consider himself a priest or clergyman, nor did John start any churches, Bible colleges, or charitable foundations. He wasn't considered a great leader with grand oratorical skills. He never amassed wealth, power, or prosperity. The Baptist had hopes and failures just as any ordinary man. He was an ordinary person who served an extraordinary God, like many of you who are reading this.

Why did masses of people come to hear John speak? Jesus asked the people of Israel the same question. "What did you go to the wilderness to see? A blade of grass blowing in the wind? What did you go to see? A handsome man in fine clothes? What did you go out to see?" The people of Israel realized John was a prophet and knew he preached the truth. They didn't want to hear a watered down message from one who feared men's opinions. They didn't come to hear someone who wanted the praise of men. They came from miles around because they were hungry for the truth. They wanted to hear a word from God. Their spiritual senses were developed enough to know something big was about to break forth and they knew the Baptist played an integral part.

Jesus publicly commended John for his faithful obedience. Speaking of the Baptist, He said, "John was a lamp that burned and gave light, and you chose for a time to enjoy his light (John 5:35)." John the Baptist overcame and loved not his life unto death (Revelation 12:11). King Herod beheaded the Baptist for preaching the truth. John the Baptist was a great preacher of righteousness. Did Israel heed the Baptist's warnings? For a few brief years when John and Jesus were preaching, Israel experienced revival. As we have seen, many people came out in the wilderness to hear John, including many Pharisees. The Bible says many repented and were baptized. John had disciples, some of whom later followed Jesus. Because of John's preaching many were more willing to hear Jesus with expectation.

Just a short time later, we see what's in the heart of man. John was thrown in prison and later beheaded after only about a year of public ministry. And Jesus, the long awaited Messiah was crucified after only about three years of public ministry. The Messiah's crucifixion quenched the fires of revival for many in Israel who refused to believe that Christ had risen from the dead. Their hopes dashed, their enthusiasm quickly turned into disappointment since they were expecting only an earthly kingdom from the Messiah and it didn't transpire. Because of this deception, many in Israel missed their hour of visitation (Luke 19:44). They misunderstood God's purpose for Jesus coming to earth.

As a result, much of Israel refused to believe Christ was God's Son and had risen from the dead. Only a small remnant of disciples was on hand to see the resurrection of Christ.

At the same time, a seed was planted which was to bring a great harvest for God's kingdom. On the Day of Pentecost, when the Holy Spirit came upon Jesus' disciples as a rushing mighty wind, the early church grew in Jerusalem. When Christ's disciples fell into much persecution from the ultraorthodox Jews, the church was scattered. With the Apostles Peter and Paul leading the way, the Church went unto the Gentile nations. The world was never the same.

Still, Israel for the most part, failed to heed John the Baptist's warnings. They couldn't overcome their preconceived ideas that the Messiah would come and overthrow the Roman Empire. Hence, they didn't believe that Jesus was the true Messiah. In the year 70 AD, God's judgment fell upon the Jews. The Roman Legion came and destroyed the temple, just as Jesus prophesied. Many Jews were slaughtered by the Roman army. The Jews were scattered throughout the earth, just as the prophets foretold. And the Baptist's stark warnings became reality:

> The ax is already at the root of the trees, and every tree that does not produce good fruit will be cut down and thrown into the fire.
> —Luke 3:9

Chapter 6

FRIENDS OF GOD

GOD USUALLY CHOSE men and women whom the world disdained. They were often made fun of. They were considered weak or uneducated. Those who were educated or wealthy were still ostracized by much of their society for believing in Christ and living the Spirit-filled life. Some gave their fortunes away to follow Christ. They were considered strange, cults, or radical extremists. Many were outcasts of the world, treated with contempt and disrespect; imprisoned or forced to wander in the desert and the wilderness.

God chose ordinary, weak men and women so He'd receive all the glory. He anointed them with His Spirit of wisdom and grace. Realizing their own personal weaknesses apart from God, these men and women learned to depend on Him to accomplish the tasks before them.

We can see this truth in the celebration of our Savior's birth. The Wise men weren't prominent citizens of Israel, but foreigners who came from afar. They laid aside their traditions and prejudices to seek the Lord. They received insight and revelation from God. Filled with God's wisdom, they followed the star and found a babe wrapped in cloth lying in a manger; the Son of God who is to rule and reign forever.

The angels announced the King's birth, not to nobles or leaders, but to shepherds tending their flocks. What an honor to be among the first to know of our Savior's birth. The shepherds obviously were God's friends. The angels announced to the shepherds, God's plans to save not only Israel, but all of mankind through the Messiah that was born.

God revealed the Messiah not to the temple priests, but to an old man named Simeon, a righteous and devout man who was looking forward to the Messiah. Guided by the Spirit, he entered the temple while Mary and Joseph were there dedicating their firstborn son to God. Simeon recognized the baby as the Anointed One. God had revealed the Messiah to Simeon rather than to the temple priests.

> Then Simeon blessed them and said to Mary, his mother: "This child is destined to cause the falling and rising of many in Israel, and to be a sign that will be spoken against so that the thoughts of many hearts will be revealed. And a sword will pierce your own soul too."
> —Luke 2:34-35

Instead of the wealthy, God revealed the Messiah to a poor widow. For 84 years Anna had been a widow. She lived at the temple complex, serving God with fasting and prayers. She also was able to see the baby Jesus and thanked God for Him. She began to speak about Him to all who were looking forward to the redemption of Jerusalem (Luke 2:36-38).

Securing the Insecure

Moses was called to lead God's people from the bondage of harsh slavery. Raised in the household of Pharaoh, Moses sensed this destiny upon his life. He seemed drawn back to his Jewish roots; drawn to the Hebrew's God. One day Moses became angry with the Egyptians' harsh treatment of the Hebrew slaves and killed an Egyptian overseer. Because of his pride and inability to control his anger, Moses took matters into his own hands rather than patiently waiting for God's instructions. As a result, He was forced to flee into the wilderness to avoid Pharaoh's wrath. He remained in the desert for forty years, his divine destiny all but forgotten.

But what God ordains, he brings to pass. God wouldn't allow Moses to run from his calling or to give up. Unaware by Moses, God was preparing him in the desert wilderness to return to Egypt and lead His people to freedom. God caught his attention with the burning bush. By this time, Moses had all but forgotten about his sense of destiny. Once a mighty prince of Egypt, Moses was humbled by his many years in the desert as a shepherd. He now saw himself as somewhat of a failure. The distinguished life of royalty he had once lived in Egypt as the son of Pharaoh's daughter seemed to him only a vague memory of shattered dreams. God confronted Moses at the burning bush and appointed him to lead His people out of bondage. I believe as God spoke with Moses at the burning bush, Moses was filled with the Spirit and God anointed him with wisdom to do the task before him.

At first, this seemed too radical for Moses to believe. By now, he had become comfortable as a shepherd. He had found contentment in a simple life in the wilderness. After leaving his powerful position as the son of Pharaoh's daughter, he was satisfied with being a shepherd in the wilderness. Moses was no longer subjected to the pressure and sober responsibility as one of Egypt's royalty. After his tragic blunder in Egypt, he became somewhat insecure. No longer was he the bold respected prince of Egypt, but an ordinary man of the wilderness with a family to support. He no longer saw himself as a deliverer, but only a shepherd. He was content to live out his life in the desert with the sheep.

As a matter of fact, Moses became so insecure he began to stutter. His opinion of himself became so low he couldn't imagine himself as a leader. He stuttered and made a futile attempt with God to get out of his mission. The Bible states Moses was the meekest of all the earth. God had worked with Moses to bring him from the arrogance of royalty to the humility of a shepherd, far away in the wilderness. He asked God to let his brother, Aaron, speak on his behalf.

As God spoke to Moses in the desert wilderness, he learned to accurately discern God's voice. God spoke to Moses face to face as a man speaks with his friend (Exodus 33:11). Despite Moses' insecurity and weaknesses, God used him to birth what is now the nation of Israel and to become one of the most well known leaders of all time; because he believed God.

Mighty Man of Valor

Gideon didn't see himself as a leader or deliverer of Israel. Like Moses, he seemed to be an insecure man. The Angel found him hiding from the Midianites. God's Angel came to Gideon and told him to go and save Israel from the Midianites' hand. By faith the angel called Gideon a mighty man of valor. God can see in us things we cannot see. He sees though the eyes of faith. God saw in Gideon the potential of a great leader, a man of faith who would obey and lead the people to a great victory over the Midianites.

> "But sir," Gideon replied, "if the LORD is with us, why has all this happened to us? Where are all his wonders that our fathers told us about when they said, 'Did not the LORD bring us up out of Egypt?' But now the LORD has abandoned us and put us into the hand of Midian."
>
> —Judges 6:13

Gideon had become so accustom to the Israelites' bondage by the Midianites, he had trouble believing the angel.

> The LORD turned to him and said, "Go in the strength you have and save Israel out of Midian's hand. Am I not sending you?"
>
> —Judges 6:14

But Gideon saw himself only though the natural. Gideon began to make excuses.

> "But Lord," Gideon asked, "how can I save Israel? My clan is the weakest in Manasseh, and I am the least in my family."
>
> —Judges 6:15

The Lord assured Gideon He'd be with him. Still unable to understand why God chose him with all of his weaknesses, Gideon began to doubt. Was the Angel really from God, or from his own imagination? To bolster his insecurity, Gideon asked for a sign. It was only when God gave him a supernatural sign that Gideon decided to obey. God continued to reassure him. He trained him and prepared him for war. Gideon went on to supernaturally defeat the vast army of Midianites with only 300 men. Afterwards, he successfully ruled and judged Israel for his remaining lifetime. Time after time God used ordinary men and women to accomplish extraordinary feats; and the list continues. Think of men and women whom God used just in American history; how our founding fathers accomplished sacrificial exploits to birth a great nation. What about the men and women throughout history who did great things for God, but were never recorded in the Bible? Although unrecorded in the Bible or history books, these men and women of God are recorded in the Lamb's Book of Life.

Let's look at a few examples of how God worked around the mistakes of some of these ordinary heroes to accomplish eternal things.

Chapter 7

TURNING FAILURES INTO SUCCESSES

"BY FAITH ABRAHAM, when called out to a place where he would later receive as his inheritance, obeyed and went, even though he didn't know where he was going" (Hebrews 11:8). After Abraham began his journey of faith, a famine came upon the land. He went down to Egypt during the famine. Abraham realized his wife was very beautiful. He feared the Egyptians would kill him in order to take his wife. Apparently, it wasn't uncommon in ancient days for men to kill in order to steal another man's wife. Before the Law, most men knew little of God's righteous standards. Abraham was so fearful of the Egyptians, he instructed his wife, Sarah, to pretend she was his sister. Keep in mind that when God told Abraham to leave his family, He promised to make Abraham a great nation (Genesis 12:2). How could Abraham become a great nation if he were murdered before having any offspring? Fear caused Abraham to doubt God's promise.

In spite of this, God knew Abraham would continue to grow stronger in faith. God told Abraham He would make him the father of nations, and Abraham believed Him. God eventually changed his name from Abram to Abraham, meaning the father of many nations.

Later Abraham moved to the land of the Negev. Again he became fearful the men of the land would kill him to obtain Sarah, so he hid the fact Sarah was his wife. But God forgave Abraham for his momentary lapse of faith. God sees the big picture; not just what we are at this present moment, but what we can become as He crafts us into His beautiful masterpiece. Despite Abraham's weaknesses, God still fulfilled His promise to him. God had made a covenant with Abraham and He doesn't break His Word.

Again Abraham, having taken Sarah's advice, relied on his own understanding instead of waiting on God with faith and patience. He took matters into his own hand and fathered a son, Ishmael, through his wife's Egyptian servant thinking this would be the promised son.

But God didn't give up on Abraham and worked all these blunders for his good (Romans 8:28). Abraham continued to grow in faith, power, wealth, and favor. Ishmael went on to become a great nation, even though he wasn't the promised son.

Abraham and Sarah eventually had the promised son, Isaac. As he continued to walk with God, Abraham became strong in faith. When God tested him, he was willing to obey and offer the promised son, Isaac, on the altar as a sacrifice, believing God could raise him from the dead (Hebrews 11:19). Abraham continued to grow in his faith and became known as the father of faith.

From Persecutor to Persecuted

The Apostle Paul greatly persecuted the saints believing he was doing God's will. Paul was a chief enemy of the gospel, hindering God's will for the church. He disrupted the Holy Spirit's work wherever he went, bringing havoc to the church. He thought of himself as a successful Pharisee, striving to obey the Torah and the traditions of men. He saw Christianity as a cult which opposed Judaism. He thought his attempt to end this cult was doing God a favor. Although Paul was successful in men's eyes, the truth was he was a total failure with misguided religious zeal.

On the road to Damascus, Paul had an experience with Christ that turned his life around:

> As he neared Damascus on his journey, suddenly a light from heaven flashed around him. He fell to the ground and heard a voice say to him, "Saul, Saul, why do you persecute me?" "Who are you, Lord?"

Saul asked. "I am Jesus, whom you are persecuting," he replied. "Now get up and go into the city, and you will be told what you must do."
—Acts 9:3-6

Paul obeyed Christ and preached the gospel to the gentiles. Everywhere he went the Jews stirred up trouble in an attempt to make things difficult for him. Paul perceived a messenger of Satan had been sent to buffet him. He was ridiculed, falsely accused, run out of town, beaten, and even stoned. Some Jews even followed him from town to town trying to discredit him. Satan sent storms and snakes to destroy Paul.

If this wasn't enough, Paul also faced persecution within the church. Paul apparently wasn't striking in appearance and lacked a charismatic personality. Maybe he was short and bald. From reading his letters, Paul implies he wasn't an excellent, dynamic speaker as were some of the other leaders in the church. In one of his letters to the Corinthian church, Paul wrote,

When I came to you, brothers, I did not come with eloquence or superior wisdom as I proclaimed to you the testimony about God. For I resolved to know nothing while I was with you except Jesus Christ and him crucified. I came to you in weakness and fear, and with much trembling. My message and my preaching were not with wise and persuasive words, but with a demonstration of the Spirit's power, so that your faith might not rest on men's wisdom, but on God's power.
—1 Corinthians 2:1-5

It's also inferred from Paul's letters that some of the church had failed to respect him. He worked making tents to provide his subsistence. Perhaps he didn't receive the huge offerings others leaders received (1 Corinthians 9:1-6). In his letters to the Corinthian church, he spent some time convincing them of his authority as an apostle (2 Corinthians, chapter 11). Portions of his letters reveal that some in the church failed to esteem Paul and the office to which he was called (1 Corinthians 1:12; 2 Corinthians 10:10). Others attempted to degrade Paul out of envy (Philippians 1:15-17).

Remember the words I spoke to you: "No servant is greater than his master. If they persecuted me, they will persecute you also. If they obeyed my teaching, they will obey yours also.

—John 15:20

Paul cried out three times for God to deliver him from the turmoil, but God responded, "My grace is sufficient for you, for my power is made perfect in weakness" (2 Corinthians 12:9).

Paul went on to plant churches at Rome and throughout the Middle East. The New Testament saints base much of their theology on Paul's letters to the Church. Most of these letters were written while Paul was in prison.

Christ's Apostles, with the exception of Judas, were also preachers of righteousness. They were set apart, having fellowshipped with Jesus. These were fishermen, tax collectors, and mostly uneducated men. Yet these ordinary men spoke with wisdom and power. These once ordinary men became filled with God's Spirit. They warned of judgments to come for those who reject Christ and His words. Filled with courage and boldness, they proclaimed the gospel of Jesus Christ unashamedly. The Pharisees recognized they had been with Jesus (Acts 4:13). The world will recognize those who walk with God.

Some may see preachers of righteousness as only the Old Testament prophets who lived under the Old Covenant. As we shall see from the following chapters on Finney, God called preachers of righteousness throughout the church age. Although sometimes the world and even the church don't recognize them, there are preachers of righteousness living even now in our present generation.

Part III

His Truth Is Marching On

Chapter 8

INTRODUCTION TO FINNEY

~❦◯

THE LARGE ROOM was crowded to its utmost capacity. As the congregation sang, the preacher began to pray silently on bended knees. During his prayer, the Holy Spirit gave him the subject to preach on: "The carnal mind is at enmity against God." When the congregation finished their singing, he arose and stepped to the pulpit. Like a lawyer arguing his case, he presented God's case before the people. As he explained how the carnal mind opposes the high standard of God's holiness, the people became convicted of sin. Many heads were bowed down with deep godly sorrow.

On the next day, the meeting room was again packed with people. Again, the Holy Spirit gave the preacher the subject shortly before he stepped to the pulpit. He began to address God's charges against man's unregenerate nature. The people's conviction deepened every moment. Some appeared to writhe in pain. He led the congregation in the sinner's prayer amidst the sobbing, heavy breathing, and the people's sighs. Some fainted under the Holy Spirit's convicting power, while others produced a loud shrieking or wailing. Many sinners present at the meeting were converted to Christ and went home so full of joy they could hardly contain themselves.

The story just mentioned is an account of a nineteenth century revivalist. We've studied those in the Bible who preached of righteousness and judgment; those under the old covenant who warned of judgments to come. Now, let's take a look at a preacher of righteousness under the new covenant who warned others to repent and come to Christ; one who preached on judgment and salvation in the last days.

This preacher of righteousness recorded some of his experiences in a book of memoirs. Unlike the revivalists mentioned in the Bible, we have more specifics on the content of his preaching. In this case, we have a wonderful opportunity to look into this preacher's life with far greater detail than those recorded in ancient times; his name, Charles G. Finney.

I've taken the initiative to include the resistance to the revivals conducted by Finney. As with all revival movements of the past, I believe there will be opposition to the next move of God, some which will come from church leaders. For this reason, you will see the positive aspects of Finney's revivals, as well as the opposition.

Although Finney's memoirs are over four hundred pages, it doesn't nearly cover all of the incidents of miracles and conversions for which he so faithfully labored. He convincingly asserts it would take volumes to record all of the marvelous works done in the revivals to which he was a part of. I've taken only excerpts from Finney's memoirs which relate to divine destiny, revival, and spiritual truths. Finney's memoirs mention the opposition he faced and the victories of his ministry; many wonderful conversions; God's faithfulness in the midst of trials; perseverance in the midst of afflictions.

The United States of America faced several important moral issues, much like we do today, including slavery and erroneous doctrines. During this time, Charles Finney emerged as a leading spokesman for God, during a movement which brought revival to the nation.

Chapter 9

CALLED AND CHOSEN

BORN IN WARREN, Connecticut in 1792, God began to prepare Finney for his destiny. Like many preachers of righteousness, his parents weren't ministers or professors of religion. He was the youngest of fifteen children. As a young person he had musical skills and leadership abilities. Growing up in the frontier of New York, he seldom heard a gospel sermon from anyone. He had very little interest in the churches or religion of his day.

Since most American schools of the nineteenth century taught from the Bible, Finney did have a limited knowledge of God. Occasionally a traveling minister came to town, or an uneducated person held meetings in the wilderness where he lived. However, he noticed many of these ministers seemed to know less of the Bible than he. Some probably couldn't even read, so he looked upon them with disdain as he listened to the error and strange absurdities some preachers presented. Of considerable intelligence, he recognized their error in doctrine even though he wasn't fully convinced the Bible was true.

As he grew older he showed more interest in the Bible and attended church meetings when possible. God was drawing him, grooming him to make a difference in his generation. Finney moved to New Jersey where he taught school. He also trained in legal studies while he worked at a law office. He had many questions, and debated with some of the ministers concerning their positions on certain truths. God later used Finney's debating skills to contend for the truth and to expose error in the church.

He was skeptical of some ministers because he noticed their prayers for an outpouring of God's Spirit never seemed to be answered. Nevertheless, he read Jesus' words, "Ask and it shall be given. Seek and you shall find. Knock and it shall be opened unto you." He came to the conclusion either these ministers were missing it or the Bible wasn't true. As he continued to search the scriptures, his eyes were opened.

Finney's Conversion

In his own words Finney describes his new found revelation, "But on further reading of my Bible, it struck me that the reason why their prayers weren't answered was because they didn't comply with the revealed conditions upon which God had promised to answer prayer, that they didn't pray in faith in the sense of expecting God to give them the things that they asked for."[3] These ministers prayed for revival, then talked in negative unbelief. They negated their prayers with their unbelieving conversations. They weren't expecting a great outpouring of God's Spirit. Therefore, they were receiving what they believed and spoke. This revelation on faith eventually led to his conversion to Christ.

Finney wrestled with the decision to surrender his life to Christ. One night having become nervous about putting off his decision, he had trouble sleeping. He describes a strange feeling coming over him as if he were about to die. He knew if he died that night, he'd awake in hell. He became very anxious for his soul to the point of screaming, but managed to quiet himself until morning. At this point in his life, Finney began to distinguish God's voice:

> In the morning I rose, and at an early hour started for the office. But just before I arrived at the office something seemed to confront me with questions like these. Indeed, it seemed as if the inquiry was within myself, as if an inward voice said to me, "What are you waiting for? Did you not promise to give your heart to God? And what are you trying to do? Are you endeavoring to work out a righteousness of your own?"[4]

At that moment, Finney decided he'd wait no longer. On his way to the office, he took a detour down a familiar trail where he often went to be alone. He left the trail and went into the woods, got on his knees, and surrendered his life to Christ. He saw he couldn't obtain salvation by his own righteousness, but only by the atonement of Christ. Only by taking on God's righteousness through Christ, could he receive eternal life. Finney realized instead of obtaining righteousness by his own efforts, he must accept it as a gift. The death of Christ gives us life. The suffering of Christ allows us to receive healing. The blood of Christ brings us forgiveness. He prayed in the woods all morning and God's promises began to flow into his mind from the scriptures. He finally left the woods to attend to his duties at the office.

After the law office closed, Finney decided to build a fire and stay for the evening. His law firm partner having left, Finney went to the back part of the office. As Finney describes the scene, God's presence filled the office:

> As I went in and shut the door after me, it seemed as if I met the Lord Jesus Christ face to face … and saw Him as I would see any other man. He said nothing, but looked at me in such a manner as to break me right down at His feet. I have always since regarded this as a most remarkable state of mind, for it seemed to me a reality that He stood before me and that I fell down at His feet and poured out my soul to Him.[5]

After this marvelous experience, Finney returned to the front part of the office to find the fire he built had nearly died. But a fire began to burn in his belly. It was the Holy Spirit's fire. As if his previous wonderful experience wasn't enough, God had more for this preacher of righteousness. That evening, without expecting it, Finney received the Baptism in the Holy Spirit. Finney later wrote how he could feel the impression, like a wave of electricity, going through and through his body and soul. He described it as waves of liquid love; as God's very breath.

Like Enoch, Noah, Elijah, and John the Baptist, Charles Finney walked with God. Even before he surrendered his life to Christ, God was preparing Finney for his destiny. He taught him to hear His voice. All men and women who made an impact in their generation learned to hear and obey the Shepherd's voice. All of them placed great value on fellowshipping with their creator.

> Remain in me, and I will remain in you. No branch can bear fruit by itself; it must remain in the vine. Neither can you bear fruit unless you remain in me. I am the vine; you are the branches. If a man remains in me and I in him, he will bear much fruit; apart from me you can do nothing.
> —John 15:4-5

Launch into the Deep

Finney began preaching the gospel with immediate success. The early years of his walk with Christ were spent in much prayer and meditation in the Word. He groaned and travailed in prayer on behalf of certain sinners and saw their lives changed through the power of Christ. Finney spoke in truth and power, his words penetrating the hearts of many, leaving a lasting impression of righteousness. Several friends and acquaintances were converted and healed.

In answering God's call upon his life, he placed himself under the Presbytery's care as a candidate for ministry. As Finney walked with God and meditated on the scriptures, he began to notice how some of what was being taught at his church didn't line up with the scriptures. He applied the same principals for interpreting the scriptures, as he did for his law books, which turned out to be sound homiletics. Accordingly, he noticed several discrepancies between the Bible and some of the theological doctrines of his church. For this reason he declined when some of his colleagues urged him to go to Princeton to study theology. He frankly told them they had been wrongly educated and these doctrines weren't what he believed ministers of Christ should be teaching.

Like other preachers of righteousness, Finney faced much opposition and persecution. Of this opposition Finney stated, "Purer and more powerful revivals of religion I never saw than those that have been most spoken against."[6] Like Jesus, much of the opposition to Finney's revivals came from the established religious leaders and theologians.

Some expressed their desire to prohibit him from preaching until he obtained a proper ministerial education. They felt he brought down the dignity of the pulpit and the profession. Consequently, he very seldom felt accepted by them. To them, he was a man who had entered the ministry without the proper training. He didn't fit into their mold of what constituted a minister. When he first received his minister's license, the pastor assigned to train Finney had less than an admirable opinion of him. He remarked after Finney had preached for his church, he'd be ashamed for others to know Finney had studied theology under him. Years, later, this minister asked Finney to lead him to salvation, apparently having never been converted.

Finney believed the seminaries of his generation crippled the minister's usefulness. He challenged traditional beliefs taught in the Presbytery, which he proved were misinterpretations of the scriptures. On the other hand, some of the clergy challenged his methods of preaching because he didn't attend one of the theological seminaries. Finney simply compared the results. There were very few, if any, sinners being converted under the ministry of those theologians who criticized him. On the contrary, revival resulting in many changed lives was evident wherever Finney preached. To Finney, an attorney by trade, the evidence proved his method and manner of preaching was the right one.

Instead of written sermons of eloquence and vocabulary not understood by the common people, he preached extemporaneously. While most preachers of his day read their sermons from written work prepared days, or perhaps even months before, Finney relied on the Holy Spirit to give him a message for a particular congregation at that specific time.

The Spirit of Prayer

Charles Finney was a man of prayer. His sermons were born in prayer. There were also many others who prayed for his revivals, including a large number of women. A man named Abel Clary, having been converted in the same revival as Finney, was a licensed minister. However, the Spirit of prayer was so mightily upon him, he wasn't able to preach much. Most of his time and strength was given to prayer for the souls of men. He would travel to the same location where Finney was conducting his revivals and was so burdened for souls, he was unable to come to any of the meetings, but continually prayed as long as Finney was preaching the revival. He would groan and travail in prayer for hours.

Father Nash referred to by his friends as Brother, earnestly prayed for the revivals as well. There were several others mentioned by Finney who had the same powerful Spirit of prayer. With the travailing prayer of these saints going forth and Finney's fiery sermons, they were a formidable team for revival.

Everywhere Finney traveled, the Spirit of prayer came upon the people. Even the new converts spent hours in prayer for lost souls. The remarkable results of Finney's revivals weren't just because of Finney's labors. Others labored as well and spread the word concerning the revivals. New converts, zealous for God's kingdom, shared their testimonies with the lost souls and brought them to the revival meetings.

In Philadelphia there was a tract of land in the northern part of Pennsylvania referred to as the lumber region. Many lumberjacks lived and worked in the lumber region. The land was unsettled, except for the lumbermen and their families. There were no schools or churches in the region. Cut off from the outside due to the nature of their work, many of these men were uneducated and had never read the Bible. During the spring, when the Delaware River was high, they'd transport their lumber by raft down the river to Philadelphia.

Some of these men attended Finney's revival while in Philadelphia and were converted to Christ. They returned to the wilderness and began praying for revival in the lumber region. They told their neighbors about the meetings in Philadelphia and shared with them the gospel of salvation through Jesus Christ. Their efforts met with great success and revival began to spread among the lumbermen. God's Spirit moved in such a mighty way upon the region, some were convicted without even hearing a sermon or testimony. Some repented and were converted without ever having attended a church meeting!

On occasions, Finney had no idea what he was going to preach until he stood behind the pulpit. He'd get on his knees in prayer during the worship time and receive the sermons minutes before he preached. He trusted the Holy Spirit to give him divine inspiration.

> But make up your mind not to worry beforehand how you will defend yourselves. For I will give you words and wisdom that none of your adversaries will be able to resist or contradict.
>
> —Luke 21:14-15

He gave illustrations that were understood by the common people. His sermons weren't just fine rhetorical arguments, but truths which transformed lives. He spoke words of divine power piercing the hearts of people, so they did not soon forget. Instead of praising the minister for his eloquent sermon, those present in the congregation gave praise to God for the changed lives. He didn't try to make an impression upon the people of what a good orator he was. He preached with a fervency and fire which demanded that people make a decision. He identified with the Apostle Paul when Finney wrote he was not taught by men, but by God's Spirit, Himself (Galatians 1:11-12).

Chapter 10

RIGHTLY DIVIDING THE WORD

AS IN EVERY generation, there were erroneous doctrines within the established church organizations. Some of these erroneous doctrines weren't exactly heresy, but simply a misinterpretation of scriptures by well meaning theologians and ministers. Many well intended ministers adhered to these erroneous doctrines which Finney believed prevented multitudes from coming into a saving knowledge of Christ. Indeed, some of these ministers later found they, themselves, had never actually been converted to Christ. Because these erroneous teachings caused deception among the people, preventing them from salvation, Finney felt one of the purposes for his calling was to expose these errors which had been taught and accepted in the church for years.

Interpreting the scriptures shouldn't be mystic or difficult, but requires the Holy Spirit's wisdom. God created logic and common sense for accurate communication. Having studied law, the Holy Spirit prepared Finney for the proper interpretation of scriptures. God is a God of logic. He is wisdom. If we're one of His children, He has given us His wisdom. His logic goes beyond man's logic and human understanding. Many errors in interpretation of the scriptures come by adding meanings that aren't really there, or omitting scriptures because of unbelief.

For example, let's examine the scripture in the gospel according to Mark. The previous day Jesus had cursed a fig tree. The next day as

He and his disciples walked by, they noticed the fig tree had dried up and died. His disciples marveled at the authority of Jesus' words. Jesus went on to say:

> I tell you the truth, if anyone says to this mountain, "Go, throw yourself into the sea," and does not doubt in his heart but believes that what he says will happen, it will be done for him. Therefore I tell you, whatever you ask for in prayer, believe that you have received it, and it will be yours.
>
> —Mark 11:23-24

The logical interpretation of this scripture based on what Jesus said, as well as the entire New Testament concerning faith, is about the power in our words. First, we must find the will of God on the matter, based on the Bible and leading of the Holy Spirit. If we're abiding in Christ we'll know His will for the situation. Once we know His will and we don't doubt in our hearts, then we, as His disciples, can ask and it shall be done. If we're abiding in Christ, and He's abiding within us, our desires will be His desires (John 15:7). Since His Word is abiding within us, we'll not ask for something contrary to the scriptures or contrary to His will. If we aren't abiding in Christ, we may ask with self-centered motives that conflict with God's will, and God will not hear such prayers.

Some misinterpret or discredit this scripture because of unbelief. They interpret this scripture as symbolic rather than literal. Perhaps they have no understanding of the authority Jesus gave to His disciples; the power in our words and what we say. Maybe, they tried asking and it didn't work for them or they asked with wrong motives (James 4:3). Our experiences don't make Jesus' words void. Just because someone claims they tried Mark 11:23 and it didn't work, it doesn't relegate Jesus' words to some mystic symbolism. Jesus meant what He said. If we abide in Him, find His will on the matter, and don't doubt in our hearts, we can have whatever we say. In addition, whatever we say under the authority of Christ will be done.

Others misinterpret scriptures due to self-centered or sinful motives. God will never give us something contrary to His written Word, no matter how much we confess and believe. He will never grant us someone else's spouse. Nor would He give us a million dollars if our motive is to consume it just for selfish motives.

Sometimes, we tend to interpret the scriptures from our preconceived ideas rather than approaching the Bible with childlike humility and trust. When we walk by faith we can't always rely on man's logic. On the other hand, God created logic. The reason some men see God's ways as illogical is because God's logic is infinitely higher than man's. Principles of logic, such as inductive and deductive reasoning can be used to interpret the scriptures. Proper interpretation requires we read a scripture in context with the preceding and following scriptures, as well as the whole Bible. We also must read the Bible in faith. It's when one strays away from these logical principles of interpretation that error can occur.

Some refuse to use logical interpretation because of unbelief, some due to selfish motives, and others because they have a preconceived idea of what they want or think the Bible should say. Some try to force the Bible to conform to their preconceived ideas of Jesus. For instance, some don't want to see Jesus as the Just Messiah who is coming to judge the earth and punish all the ungodly. Some Bible teachers only want to see Christ as the Lamb, but totally ignore Christ as the Lion. Our Messiah came as a meek Lamb to take away our sin. But, He's returning as a mighty Lion to crush His enemies; to rule and reign. The theologians' preconceived ideas explain why some study the Bible for years without attaining knowledge of the truth.

Many erroneous teachings Finney challenged still exist today in the form of Universalism, Unitarianism, and Calvinism.

Universalism

Finney exposed the error of Universalism which teaches there is more than one way to heaven and all men will eventually be saved. A philosophy which began in the eighteenth century, Universalism was a widespread erroneous doctrine in the church by the time of the nineteenth century. Finney noticed how the unrepentant seemed to flock to hear a Universalist preacher in his town. Consequently, Finney based a person's true conversion to Christ, not on just a person's claim to be a Christian, but also on genuine repentance. On one occasion, he challenged the doctrines of a Universalist preacher and declared that if he couldn't show the Universalist's views to be false, he'd become a Universalist himself. He lectured about the subject using his legal training to argue his case and proved to the satisfaction of all present that Universalism was based upon a false interpretation of the scriptures. Many Universalists were converted through Finney's preaching.

Universalists are even more widespread today. Elements of Universalism can be found in the modern New Age movement—the belief there are many religions and paths to God. This great lie will be a central doctrine of the one world religion within the One World Order, over which the Antichrist will rule. In the name of tolerance, this religion will encourage lawlessness. It will tolerate all religions and all people except for the true believers; those who believe the Bible is literally God's inspired Word; that Christ was born of a Virgin and rose from the dead; those who remain unstained by the world system.

Unitarianism

Unitarianism denies the existence of hell. It refuses to believe in judgment and eternal punishment. These errors result because the clergy and people don't want to receive anything from God's inspired Word which they deem as being "negative." Many Universalists take the word of some Bible teachers, without closely examining the scriptures with an open mind to discern its intent. Unitarians omit scriptures in the Bible that refer to repentance, hell, judgment, or punishment. Finney would later encounter Unitarianism often, especially in Boston. He describes how this erroneous belief had gotten such a stronghold in Boston. The majority there were more unsettled in their beliefs than any other place in which he preached. He went on to say the Unitarian influence had made it extremely difficult for them to receive the truth because they denied the Bible's principal doctrines. The apostle Paul warned of such in his second letter to Timothy:

> They are the kind who worm their way into homes and gain control over weak-willed women, who are loaded down with sins and are swayed by all kinds of evil desires, *always learning but never able to acknowledge the truth.*
>
> —2 Timothy 3:6-7

Finney describes their doctrine as one of denials; a negative theology. In Finney's mind, this opened them up to all kinds of crazy and irrational views on religion; in his own words, "They deny almost everything, and affirm almost nothing."[7]

The influence of Unitarianism today may be more prevalent than even Universalism in our society. Some, even within the church, believe because God is love, He wouldn't send anyone to hell. They fail to realize God's very nature of love and justice moved Him to prepare a hell. God must banish the rebellious from His presence to protect His covenant people from being destroyed by evil. His righteous perfection requires eternal punishment to satisfy justice. Some today have no sense of true justice.

Some clergymen and Bible teachers no longer believe God inflicts men with eternal punishment. Although some stop just short of Unitarianism, they imply God doesn't bring judgment to the nations or to His church. They reason with human logic, "God doesn't punish people." On the contrary, in the Apostles' letters to the church, they indicate frequently that God will punish the ungodly, as well as His own people in the church who rebel or live a carnal lifestyle. He chastises those whom He loves (Hebrews 12:5-11).

The truth is we bring our own destruction when we rebel against God. He will withdraw His presence and protection allowing Satan, the destroyer, to come. Some believe the deception that God will never destroy people, armies, or nations to bring about justice and protect His covenant people. Whether God allows destruction through the laws of the universe, through ordering His angels, or speaking His Word, He continues to rule with justice and mercy. As we see judgments unfolding upon the nations in our present generation, and as the final Day of Judgment approaches, the Unitarian belief that God doesn't punish proves to be a great lie.

Calvinism

Calvinism teaches a doctrine of "unconditional election," which asserts that God chose or predestined from eternity those whom He will bring to himself. God chooses the elect not based on the faith of people, but based on his mercy alone. This doctrine in effect nullifies man's responsibility for making a conscious decision to surrender to Christ and trust in faith for salvation. It puts all the responsibility on God. Borrowing beliefs of Augustine, this doctrine teaches that people aren't by nature inclined to love God. As a result, they are morally unable to choose Christ through their own will, because of their sinful nature.

Within Finney's denomination at that time, there were erroneous doctrines of predestination. Referred to by Finney as the Princeton theology or old order Presbytery, this deception implied man had no choice or control of his destiny. Since God was sovereign, God, not the individual, determined whether he'd accept Christ. This erroneous doctrine enabled some who embraced it to continue their sinful lifestyles, while placing the blame on God because He didn't choose them as one of the elect ones. Hence, there were many souls during the time of Finney who attended church meetings, but never experienced a genuine conversion to Christ.

Due to this misguided doctrine, it was taught that repentance wasn't a voluntary, but an involuntary change. Therefore, one couldn't repent on his own accord, but must do his duty and pray for repentance. Finney spent much time correcting this fallacy in the church. He stressed although the Holy Spirit worked in the heart of a sinner to convict him and persuade him to repent, repentance was the sinner's choice, not God's. Instead of trying to gain repentance through self-righteous works, it comes by faith. Finney taught repentance can come immediately by an act of faith in the atoning work of Christ; not through outward actions, but by a changed heart.

> For he says, "In the time of my favor I heard you, and in the day of salvation I helped you." I tell you, now is the time of God's favor, now is the day of salvation.
>
> —2 Corinthians 6:2

The idea of predestination as mentioned by the Apostle Paul in Romans 8:29-30 doesn't mean God has chosen a few elite for heaven before the world began and rejected the rest of mankind to hell. If everyone is already predestined to heaven or hell when we're born, there'd be no reason for faith in Christ. For those who are predestined for hell, it'd be futile to even attempt to believe in Christ. This doctrinal error on the one hand breeds doubt, unbelief and hopelessness for one who is convinced they're predestined for hell. On the other hand, it causes false security for those who never repent because they believe they're already predestined for heaven.

God knows the future. He knew ahead of time how man would fall under the curse and predestined His Son before the world's foundation to die on the cross for our sins. So when Paul says to the Ephesians, "In Him we are chosen, having been predestined," he is saying in essence that God chose or predestined a plan of redemption through the death of His Son and gave everyone a choice to receive or reject His plan. *He knew or predestined beforehand who'd receive His plan of salvation.* God knew you before the world's foundation. He also knew you would receive His gift of salvation. In this sense we are the chosen ones predestined in Christ to reign with Him (Ephesians 1:4-12).

Predestination means to determine beforehand. God has determined beforehand a wonderful plan for each of our lives, a plan that will honor Him and benefit mankind. His plan for our lives will bring true joy and contentment. However, it's our choice to accept or reject his predestined plan.

God is sovereign, but He chose in His sovereignty to allow man the final choice in his own destiny. His Holy Spirit moves to influence and lead those who are willing. But He'll not override our will. God's sovereignty in our lives is based on the choices we make. If we love Him and are called according to His purpose, His sovereignty is working all things for our good (Romans 8:28).

Many ministers of Finney's generation reasoned it was already predestined who'd enter God's kingdom. Therefore, they had no power to influence the lives of lost souls. Because of this doctrine, Finney's contemporaries didn't bother with aggressively preaching the gospel and winning souls.

Finney also found many lost souls convinced that since they weren't the ones chosen from eternity, it was no use to try and convert to Christ. Finney strongly opposed this doctrine, believing it prevented multitudes from converting to Christ.

So while Finney spoke of the marvelous grace of redemption through Jesus Christ, he also warned of eternal consequences if one rejected the gift of redemption. With the Holy Spirit's wisdom and power, he debated with other ministers, exposing their error. Unable to match Finney's wisdom, those who taught these erroneous doctrines resorted to personal attacks. Despite this, the fires of revival spread on. Multitudes repented and converted to Christ. Many experienced the joy and peace of forgiveness.

Characteristics of True Revival

Some in the church today frown on anyone who questions their doctrines or beliefs. They label anyone who may disagree with them as being cynical; a fault finder; one who stirs up strife. There is nothing wrong with a good debate over certain doctrines or beliefs within the church when done in good will and with the Holy Spirit's help. Indeed, some debating is necessary to obtain knowledge of the truth. Jesus debated with the Pharisees. Finney certainly believed in debating and used his skills as a lawyer to argue his case for the truth. Like Jesus and the Apostle Paul, Finney was a defender of the truth.

He taught the necessity of repentance, a radical change of heart, and justification by faith. He also stressed sanctification by faith and persistence in a holy lifestyle as evidence of salvation. Many who were converted at Finney's meetings experienced the wonderful salvation of freedom through Christ, no longer bound by sin. Their conversions weren't weak, half-hearted, insincere, and empty promises to God, but clear, strong, zealous, and enduring.

Answering his critics who accused him of causing division and making people angry, he defended the revivals. He argued it wasn't revivals which made people angry. Rather, people were naturally angry on the subject of religion. He went on to say true revivals restored man's relationship with God. In his memoirs, Finney listed the characteristic of the revivals:

1. The prevalence of a mighty Spirit of prevailing prayer.
2. Overwhelming conviction of sin.
3. Sudden and powerful conversions to Christ.

4. Great love and abounding joy of the converts.
5. Intelligence and stability of the converts.
6. Their great earnestness, activity, and usefulness in their prayers and labors for others.[8]

One of the key reasons revival followed Finney wherever he went was because he taught strictly truth from the Bible. He didn't rely on men's traditions, denominational doctrines, or contemporary preachers' opinions, but looked solely to the Bible for answers. As a result, he discovered misconceptions in Christian thinking of his generation; misconceptions which hindered people from coming to a knowledge of the truth. For example, some taught that God created men's sinful nature; that Christ died only for the elect and men's choices had nothing to do with salvation; men were incapable of repenting and overcoming sin by their own choice; since God is love, there is no hell or judgment, and everyone would eventually be saved.

With the Holy Spirit's help, Finney blasted away the theological errors of his time with analytical debates which presented amazing insight into the scriptures. They couldn't resist his wisdom. His deductive reasoning and persuasive arguments from the scriptures saved many from the judgment of hell and death, even ministers and theologians.

Chapter 11

THE SURRENDERED LIFE

ALTHOUGH, CHARLES FINNEY chose to marry a wife, he made it clear to her that Christ and His kingdom was his primary devotion. In 1824 he married Lydia Root Andrews. Much of the time, Mr. Finney denied himself the comforts of his wife to do the work of the ministry. Two days after he married his wife, he left her in the town of Evans' Mills to preach a revival in some small frontier towns, expecting to return within a week. The need was so great; he couldn't bear to leave the people. Determining the work of God's kingdom was more important than the enjoyment of his new bride, he sent a letter to his wife informing her he'd be spending the winter in Brownville, one of the small frontier towns, preaching to lost souls. After six months, He was finally able to return for his new bride.

On the return trip, he had to stop at a town called Le Rayville, about three miles outside of Evans' Mills, where his wife was staying, and get new horse shoes for his horse. When the people found out who he was, they begged him to stay and preach at the school house, since they didn't have a church building in town. There was such a mighty outpouring of the Holy Spirit he ended up staying and had to send someone to get his young wife. Finally, after over six months, he was reunited with his newly married wife. As with those preachers of righteousness who came before him, Finney was willing to make the necessary sacrifices for the sake of God's kingdom.

> The man who loves his life will lose it, while the man who hates his life in this world will keep it for eternal life. Whoever serves me must follow me; and where I am, my servant also will be. My Father will honor the one who serves me.
>
> —John 12:25-26

Charles Finney had learned the secret to true happiness; to lose his life for others. God greatly honored him, as Jesus promised He would. He spent much of his life traveling by horse and boat. Traveling during this time was much more toilsome than today. At times, it took a heavy toll on both Finney and his wife. Finney talks little of his family and personal life during his early years. He refers to his spouse as "precious wife," and implies she seldom complained. The rigors of Finney's labor eventually wore her down. Many years later, she succumbed to tuberculosis.

A Form of Godliness

Many young people of the 19th century were taught good morals and social etiquette by their parents and school teachers. They weren't subjected to the anti-God culture that influences our young people today. These young people didn't have the vices of our day such as coarse television shows, vulgar music lyrics, and violent video games to influence their thinking. They didn't have the vast knowledge of evil which our youth have today. In those times, the educators taught from the Bible as well as textbooks. Darwinism and agnosticism hadn't thus far taken hold of the educational system. Thus, there were some whose outward behavior resembled a Christian, since they were taught right from wrong at an early age. This became a subtle stumbling block to these youths who had managed through good moral upbringing to obtain a form of godliness. However, God doesn't just look at outward appearance, but the motives and intents of the heart.

"All a man's ways seem innocent to him, but motives are weighed by the LORD."

—Proverbs 16:2

Unless we have the Spirit of Christ living within us, we cannot adequately discern the motives and intents of our heart. Some who appear to have high character may be totally self centered. Their good works may not be led by the Spirit, but driven by pride and self-righteousness. Consequently, it wasn't unusual for Finney to encounter those with good morals, yet no knowledge of the truth. These good moral people had some difficulty believing they were sinners and needed a savior. Some seemingly moral people attended church; while at the same time having never known of justification by faith. Although they seemed righteous in their own eyes, they fell far short of God's requirements.

This righteousness from God comes through faith in Jesus Christ to all who believe. There is no difference, for all have sinned and fall short of the glory of God, and are justified freely by his grace through the redemption that came by Christ Jesus.

—Romans 3:22-24

There was one young lady whom Finney encountered whose family regarded her as almost perfect. Sarah was the eldest daughter from an amiable family. She believed her own righteousness qualified her to be a Christian. Finney worked with her with little success in an attempt to secure her conviction and conversion. She felt as though she was a good person and needn't repent of anything. Finally, a conversation with Finney brought her into deep conviction. The veil over her eyes was lifted. For the first time, she was able to see the sins and weaknesses in her life. She suddenly realized how much she needed a savior to bring her into right standing with God. After her conversion, her family saw an immediate change. She was strong in faith, discerning of truth, and obtained a supernatural power to influence her acquaintances for God's kingdom. She began to turn people's attention away from herself and to Jesus Christ, who alone is worthy of all honor.

On the other hand, Finney stressed the importance of the new nature in Christ, giving one the power to obey God. He emphasized that our moral or immoral decisions were voluntary; our decision to accept or reject the gospel was voluntary. The Holy Spirit influences by teaching, persuading, convicting, and guiding us to obedience. In other words, we aren't saved by trying to be a good moral person apart from the power of Christ. Without the Holy Spirit's wisdom, we lack understanding of what a good moral person actually is. However, once we choose to make Christ Lord of our lives by faith, He will lead us giving us power to obey God's commandments and do what is right in God's eyes, resulting in a holy lifestyle including good works.

Many who attend church in the twenty first century are deceived into believing they are alright with God, just because they believe Jesus died and rose again. Many of those who claim to be a Christian have a mental factual assent of the life, death, and resurrection of Christ, but it isn't of the heart. They want to believe in Christ and cling to their sinful lifestyle as well. This lack of repentance results in a false assurance which leads to eternal death; a deception that prevents one from a true conversion to Christianity. The Apostle James says that faith without action is dead. He states plainly that the demons also believe in God, and shudder at the thought of Him (James 2:17-19).

God's Manifested Presence

Finney didn't rely solely on his legal background, theological training, or debating skills, but on the Holy Spirit's power to persuade men. At one meeting he described the excitement as spontaneous, without any man-made effort to draw the crowds. Only a few words made the toughest men squirm in their seats with conviction, much like the Apostle Peter as recorded in the book of Acts.

> When the people heard this, they were cut to the heart and said to Peter and the other apostles, "Brothers, what shall we do?"
>
> —Acts 2:37

Finney described God's truth as a sword. God's Word cut with precision, bringing to the surface all that was impure. God's truth was spoken with such power it created a painful distress of conviction upon the congregation which seemed unendurable.

It wasn't unusual for whole towns to be converted during Finney's revivals. People from all walks of life; rich, poor, educated, uneducated, lawyers, merchants, housewives, and businessmen were converted. Word of the revivals spread to nearby towns. Such was the case in Finney's revival campaign in Rome, NY. During such revivals, the town's whole atmosphere was filled with God's manifested presence. No one could come into the village without feeling God's awesome presence in a peculiar and wonderful manner. It was often told how travelers passing through a town during Finney's revivals became deeply convicted of sin. Everywhere in town people were discussing religion and the Bible's truth. These travelers became so convicted that they'd seek someone to pray for them. One of the townspeople shared their faith and the traveler left the town having been converted to Christ.

In his memoirs, Finney recalls the story of a sheriff who resided in the nearby town of Utica. Having heard of the revival in Rome, he was very skeptical, and laughed about what was happening in Rome. One day it was necessary for him to go to Rome on a business trip as sheriff. He drove in his one-horse sleigh without anything unusual happening until he crossed what was called the old canal about one mile from the town of Rome. Finney continues the unusual story, as the sheriff later recounted to him:

> He said as soon as he crossed the old canal, an awful impression came over him, an awe so deep that he could not shake it off. He felt as if God pervaded the whole atmosphere. He said that this increased the whole way til he came to the village. He stopped at Mr. Flint's hotel, and the hostler looked just as he himself felt, as if he were afraid to speak. He went into the house, and found the gentlemen there with whom he had business. He said they were manifestly all so much impressed they could hardly attend to business. He said that several times in the course of the short time he was there, he had to arise from the table abruptly and go to the window and look out, and try to divert his attention, to keep from weeping.[9]

After his trip, the sheriff never again spoke lightly of Finney's work in Rome. Indeed, in many of Finney's meetings, there was such solemnity, such a manifested presence of the awesome God that people neither spoke nor moved, but tarried in His presence.

Chapter 12

FIRE AND RAIN

CHARLES FINNEY OFTEN spoke with a stern rebuke, while at the same time, a heart of love; with righteous indignation, yet tears of compassion. Just as Jesus drove out the money changers in the temple, Finney drove out hypocrisy and evil-thinking in the church with an anger and zeal for God's house. Many who heard his preaching accused him of severity. At the same time, they returned to hear him again because they sensed his compassion for them. Those living in sin were at first angered with conviction by his frankness in presenting the gospel. Nevertheless, many of them eventually repented and received the gospel.

> My preaching seemed to them to be something new. Indeed, it seemed to myself as if I could rain hail and love upon them at the same time; or in other words, that I could rain upon them hail in love.[10]

Charles Finney preached with such passion and power, people couldn't hear his sermons without being moved. Such passion stirred the hearers to repentance or rage. Those who chose to humble themselves and repent received the gospel. Those who rejected the gospel left in a rage. The zeal of Finney compelled people to choose. Those who received his message loved Finney. Those who rejected the truth hated and resisted him. There was no in-between, no indifference when Charles Finney came to town. Much like the Apostle Paul, he was met with opposition wherever he went. Also like Paul, he preached with astounding results. They couldn't argue with the Spirit's wisdom with which he spoke. Many of those who began opposing the revival ended up converting to Christ after the Holy Spirit's power was manifested. The Holy Spirit convicted the lost souls, bringing some to their knees with the weeping and groaning of heartfelt repentance.

The Sin that Leads to Death

However, there were rare occasions when the hearts of Finney's enemies were so hard; the Holy Spirit left them alone to their destruction. They zealously continued to oppose the revival and met with judgment. Finney recalls many accounts of how those who vehemently opposed the revivals ended up in untimely deaths, during the peak of the revivals. Having had many chances to receive the gospel, they resisted the Holy Spirit and hardened their hearts. Finney recounts such a one in the early part of his ministry.

> There was one old man in this place—I cannot recollect his name—who was not only an infidel, but a great railer of religion, and was very angry at the revival movement. I heard every day of his railing and blasphemy, but took no public notice of it. He refused altogether to attend the meeting. But in the midst of his opposition, and when his excitement was great, while sitting one morning at the table he suddenly fell out of his chair in a fit of apoplexy. A physician was immediately called, who, after a brief examination, told him he could live but a very short time; and that if he had anything to say, he must say it at once. He had just strength and time, as I was informed, to stammer out, "Don't let Finney pray over my corpse." This was the last of his opposition in that place.[11]

As we can see in this example, revivals bring both judgment and restoration. While God's manifested presence in Finney's revivals was a sweet smelling fragrance to those who humbled themselves, repented, and believed, it was the smell of death to those who resisted (2 Corinthians 2:16).

While conducting a revival campaign in New Lebanon, there was a man who became so disturbed about the revival he left town declaring he wouldn't return until the revival was over. He had only been gone a short time when he met a tragic death. Sometimes, judgment, as well as restoration, followed Finney's revivals.

> If anyone sees his brother commit a sin that does not lead to death, he should pray and God will give him life. I refer to those whose sin does not lead to death. There is a sin that leads to death. I am not saying that he should pray about that.
>
> —1 John 5:16

Nevertheless, God in His great mercy worked good out of this tragic incidence. The man's brother, a pastor by the name of Rev. Gilbert, heard of the revival and invited Finney to preach at his church in Wilmington, Delaware. From there, Finney went to Philadelphia, where his preaching produced astounding results. Many lives were changed by the gospel's power.

Although the wonderful works of God's love prevailed in Finney's campaigns, judgment also prevailed to some who hardened their hearts and resisted. The revivals led by Finney proved the fact revival entails judgment, as well as salvation.

Throughout Finney's ministry, opposition to his work arose. As the people continued to pray, God snuffed out the opposition and it died. When a person spoke against the revival, believers singled them out in prayer and they were soon converted. Sometimes, if they continued to resist, judgment came. Finney describes such an incident which occurred in the revival at Rome:

> But in this revival, as in others that I have seen, God did some terrible things in righteousness. On one Sabbath, whilst I was there, as we came out of the pulpit, and was about to leave the church, a man came in haste to Mr. Gillett and myself, and requested us to go to a certain place, saying that a man had fallen down dead there . . . Three men who had been opposing the work had met that Sabbath day and spent the day in drinking and ridiculing the work. They went on in this way until one of them suddenly fell down dead. When Mr. Gillett

arrived at the house and the circumstances were related to him, he said, "There! There is no doubt but that man had been stricken down by God, and has been sent to hell." His companions were speechless. They could say nothing, for it was evident to them that their conduct had brought upon him this awful stroke of divine indignation.[12]

Another such incident occurred in the town of Utica, NY. The Oneida Presbytery met there during a time when the fires of revival burned in Utica. One aged clergyman from Scotland who apparently had never seen a revival, made a violent speech before the Presbytery vehemently opposing the revival. It greatly shocked and grieved all the Christians who were present. They were concerned the clergyman's remarks could stifle the fires of revival.

At evening, after the meeting adjourned, some spent all night praying for God to counteract any evil influence that may result from the speech by the elder clergyman. The next morning, the Scottish clergyman was found dead in his bed. This produced a great shock and reverence among the people. As a result, the flames of revival intensified. Persons from distance towns in all directions, hearing what God was doing, came out of curiosity and wonder. Many of them were converted to Christ.

Answering the Call

One of these, a young school teacher, came out of curiosity. After arriving, Finney's sermons aroused her opposition and she became very disturbed about her spiritual state. Upon conversing with some of the townspeople, who were Christians, she couldn't believe sinners deserved to be sent to an eternal hell. The Holy Spirit continued to work powerfully in her heart.

She was able to arrange for a meeting with Finney. He explained to her that if she knew how terrible sin was, she wouldn't complain to God for sending sinners to hell. After impressing upon her the seriousness of deadly sin, he presented the gospel message of how Jesus died to take the penalty of our sin so we can be spared from eternal punishment. The sin which sentences men to eternal death, Jesus took upon Himself. God hates sin because sin brings death and destruction. Since all men have sinned, all of us deserve eternal punishment. Thank God, Jesus bore our sentence of doom. The veil was lifted as she began to see the truth. Her face became pale and she fell forward, weeping with a broken heart of repentance.

This young lady surrendered her life to Christ, and felt called to the mission field. As she was preparing for missions, she met her husband. They soon left for missionary work on the Sandwich Islands. She became a very productive missionary and was well known during her generation. She raised several sons who also became missionaries.

There were many such young women who were converted through Finney's powerful persuasion. At many revivals, beautiful young women attended, who were dressed in such a manner, as to draw attention to themselves. They were self-centered, believing everyone should give them special treatment because of their natural beauty. Their vain imaginations led them to believe they were better than everyone else; that everyone was constantly gazing at their beauty. The Holy Spirit convicted them of their pride and vanity. They became humble converts, with broken-hearted tears.

Around the same time, Mr. Finney preached at a small village nearby Utica. While there, he visited a garment factory in which his brother-in-law was at the time superintendent. The revival had made such a huge impact in the area, everyone in the factory had heard about it.

The next morning after breakfast, Finney was given a tour of the factory. As he went through the factory, he noticed there was considerable conviction among the factory workers. Just hearing of what Finney stood for and what he preached agitated many of the factory workers.

In passing through one of the rooms where a large number of young women were weaving, Finney noticed two young women staring at him and talking very earnestly among themselves. As they looked at Finney and laughed, he could tell they were very nervous at his presence. He walked slowly toward them. The thread broke in the machine, which one of the girls used. As he approached, he noticed the girl's hands were trembling, so she couldn't rethread her machine. When he came within about ten feet of her, he gazed at her with solemnity and she was overcome with conviction. She sunk down in her chair and burst into tears. In a few moments, nearly the whole room of girls was in tears.

Having heard of this, the factory owner closed the shop and allowed Finney to preach. The whole factory assembled in the mule room to hear Finney's message. Most of them, according to Finney's account, were saved.

When a person is filled with God's Spirit, one gaze of compassion can melt the hardest of hearts. One look into eyes of purity and holiness can bring the vilest of sinners to tears of repentance. God's manifest presence will stir people to action. They will either run from His presence, or humbly surrender with brokenness and tears.

Chapter 13

FAITH IN THE MIDST OF OPPOSITION

AS WORD SPREAD of Finney's revivals, opposition mounted. Some including a number of church leaders of the past movement resisted Finney just as the Jewish leaders opposed the Apostle Paul, though perhaps to a lesser degree. Unlike Paul, Finney's opposition didn't become violent, except a few rare instances of church burnings. In addition, many in the church ended their opposition years later and supported Finney after seeing the fruit of his ministry. Nevertheless, Finney, much like the Apostle Paul, faced stiff opposition wherever he went, especially at the beginning of his work.

The most damaging opposition came from other clergy and ministers. As Finney's revivals grew in notoriety, his methods were criticized by some prominent leaders of the church. Asahel Nettleton, one of the foremost evangelists of the earlier phase in the Second Great Awakening, as well as a Boston pastor and evangelical leader, Lyman Beecher, led an attack against what they termed as "new measures" conducted by Finney. Apparently, they were given erroneous information concerning Finney's methods of revival which were false and misleading.

Why did so many ministers resist the revival? I believe it was due to tradition, pride, envy, and an unyielding hardness toward the Holy Spirit. Most ministers during this time were very well educated. I am very much for education. I believe education helps one to make better choices and opens doors of opportunity, improving the quality of life. It can also help us to read and interpret the scriptures. However, some ministers with much education or Bible training can become so prideful it blinds them to the truth. Finney called these ministers dogmatic. They get so set in their theological thinking they are no longer open-minded with the interpretation of the scriptures. Yes, the Holy Spirit gives divine revelation from the scriptures, but this doesn't mean we leave our minds in the closet when we read the scriptures. Some Bible teachers and theologians are dogmatic, rather than logical when interpreting the scriptures.

This was the same problem Jesus had with the Pharisees. In spite of knowing the scriptures, they were unable to see the truth. They were unable to recognize the hour of God's visitation to Israel. Many clergy of Finney's generation gave well-known, respected teachers' opinions more weight than the actual truth within the Bible. The doctrine of their particular denomination or Bible College carried more weight than the scriptures. Finney resisted the dogma of his day when interpreting the scriptures. He used the logic and deductive reasoning he learned while training as a lawyer. At the same time he trusted in the Holy Spirit to give him understanding and to speak with power. As a result, he was able to discern the truth from the scriptures more accurately than most of his contemporaries, even though most of them had more theological training. Accordingly, he exposed many theological misconceptions of his generation.

Logic, in itself isn't evil or bad. Logic is part of God's natural laws. Logic is found in science and nature. It prevents God's universe from getting into anarchy. In God's kingdom it prevents us from getting out of balance due to misguided interpretations of the scriptures. God's created logic isn't simply intellectualism or human understanding, but logical interpretation of the scriptures based on the spiritual laws which govern God's kingdom. God's universe was set in motion with His spoken Word. His spoken Word encompasses physical and spiritual laws which govern the universe.

For instance, there are physical laws such as the laws of physics, the laws of math, and the laws of language. There are also spiritual laws, such as the Ten Commandments, judgment, the law of repentance, justification by faith, as well as sowing and reaping. We shouldn't totally disregard logic when interpreting scriptures. It's only when we try using logic without spiritual laws that we risk getting into heresy. Spiritual logic supersedes natural logic. For example, if we use only logic without the spiritual law of faith to interpret the scriptures, we'll end up in error or unbelief. On the other hand, if we use blind faith, without the logical interpretation of the scriptures, we risk strange doctrine, weirdness, and fanaticism.

Spiritual laws are found within the Constitution of the United States and within the laws of many other nations as well. Consequently, the same logical principals used to interpret the constitutions of many nations can be used to interpret scriptures, since much of these constitutions are based on spiritual laws.

Finney used the same rules of logic for interpreting the Bible as he did for interpreting the United States law. His logical preaching appealed to the professor and the uneducated, the professional and the blue collar. His reasonable persuasion on behalf of God's kingdom demolished atheists' arguments exposing their fallacies and melting their skepticism. Some theologians felt the common laity couldn't understand such logical explanation of the scriptures, but the Holy Spirit gave understanding to the masses and multitudes were converted.

Opposition from the East

By the time Finney began his revival campaign in Auburn, NY, word had spread east all the way to the New England states. Since Finney didn't have a formal degree in theology, many theologians feared the people would deem religious training unnecessary, which may encourage men to enter the ministry uneducated and unprepared. In their thinking, this would harm the colleges and theological seminaries. They failed to understand how the Holy Spirit can give wisdom and understanding to even the illiterate.

As a result, some wrote letters among themselves expressing hostility toward the revivals. In the areas where Finney had conducted revivals, no ministers opposed his work because they couldn't deny the results; multitudes of souls converted to Christ. Most of the ministers who opposed him were the ones who had never met Finney personally; those who resided in areas where Finney had yet to labor. Some came out publicly opposing Finney's work. Finney's reaction to the opposition was to ignore it and continue the work of preaching the gospel among the people.

However, some ministers led by a prominent evangelist organized efforts designed to prevent the spread of Finney's revivals. These ministers' strategy was to stop Finney's revivals from spreading east of Auburn, NY. The churches east of Auburn began to close their doors to Finney. Finney referred to it as a system of espionage designed to discredit him with mostly unfounded rumors. False rumors had spread about error being taught at the revivals, fleshly demonstrations of emotionalism, and excess. They labeled Finney as an extremist who allowed excess fanaticism in his revivals. The truth is Finney allowed the Holy Spirit freedom to lead the revivals and move upon the people. To many clergymen, the Holy Spirit's manifestation was considered as excess and fanaticism.

The pastor who invited Finney to preach in Auburn informed Finney of the mounting opposition in the Eastern United States. Shortly after he arrived at Auburn, Finney was engaged in prayer when the Lord showed him a vision of the persecution he must pass through. He trembled and shook from his head to his feet in God's awesome presence, as if he were on Mount Sinai with the lightning and thundering. He was awed and humbled as God drew nearer.

During this great manifestation, God assured Finney He would be with him and uphold him. No opposition would prevail against him. Finney wasn't to worry, but to wait for God's deliverance. This experience with God led him to be perfectly trustful, peaceful, and calm, even in the midst of great opposition. He had no ill will toward those who opposed him, but was able to maintain kind feelings toward them, knowing they had been misled. So Finney never stopped his work to answer or debate his critics. He never let this opposition sidetrack him from the work of producing true repentance, winning the lost to Christ. He stayed busy working in the harvest fields of Auburn, NY, with the result of many converts into God's kingdom.

> I felt assured that all would come out right, that my true course was to leave everything to God and keep about my work. I did so; and as the storm gathered and the opposition increased, I never for one moment

doubted how it would result. I was never disturbed by it, I never spent a waking hour thinking of it, when to all outward appearance it seemed as if all the churches of the land, except where I had labored, would unite to shut me out of their pulpits.[13]

Church Leaders Call for a Meeting

Finally a meeting was proposed to bring together the western leaders of the church, those from the west of Auburn, New York, who participated in past revivals, and the eastern leaders of the church, from eastern New York and the New England states, who had been opposing them. It wasn't Finney's theology they opposed, as much as his methods of revival. Finney had meetings of inquiry which emerged to what is today known as altar calls. He allowed ordinary believers to lead in prayer and give testimonies, even women of the church, which some frowned upon. He allowed manifestations of the Holy Spirit's convicting power, which included loud sobs, weeping, trembling, and shaking. It appeared some of the church leaders in the New England states mistook the Holy Spirit's convicting power as condemnation and complained of a bad spirit that prevailed in those revivals.

The meeting was held in an attempt to bring the two sides into a better understanding of one another. It was much like the meeting held by the early church leaders concerning circumcision. Many Jewish believers opposed Paul's methods of revival, namely he allowed Gentiles to be baptized without being circumcised. Some men came down from Judea to the church at Antioch and were teaching that unless one was circumcised, he couldn't be saved. Paul and Barnabas debated with them until finally the church at Antioch sent them, along with other leaders, to meet with the apostles and elders in Jerusalem concerning this matter.

Paul presented his case before the apostles and elders, and after much discussion, it was decided circumcision was a symbolic law, not a moral issue. Therefore, circumcision shouldn't be required of the Gentiles.

In the same way, those who opposed the revivals led by Finney were questioning his methods. They couldn't deny the results; hundreds being sincerely converted to Christ. Many of the pastors where Finney had conducted the revivals testified on Finney's behalf at this convention and refuted the charges against the revivals. The opposition was deeply moved by the testimonies. Most of the leaders left the meeting convinced there was no harm in Finney's methods of revival.

As a result, doors were opened for him to preach in the east. This convention convinced the majority of church leaders in New England who were present that Finney's revivals were indeed glorious; a genuine move of God. From this point forward, the opposition to Finney's revivals gradually, but greatly subsided.

Challenged by the News Media

At this point he went east and conducted revival campaigns in Wilmington, Delaware, Philadelphia, and Reading, Pennsylvania. There was a daily newspaper in Reading which greatly influenced the people. The editors of the newspaper were lacking in character. It wasn't unusual for them to become so intoxicated on public occasions, they had to be carried home. When Finney began preaching, the editors took it upon themselves to begin giving religious advice. They began to speak against Finney and the revival through their daily newspaper. This confused and perplexed many of the people. This went on from day to day, until finally Finney felt it necessary to address it.

In his next meeting, which was filled to capacity, he took for his text, "Ye are of your father the devil, and the lusts of your father ye will do." He exposed how sinners are used to fulfill the desires of the devil; how Satan sometimes speaks through people at certain times. He gave examples how people are sometimes unknowingly used by Satan and related his text to the newspaper editors, claiming they were being used by the devil to hinder God's work. He then asked the congregation if it was right for men of the editors' character to attempt to give religious instruction to the people in regard to what is right and wrong. Finney insisted if he lived in Reading, he wouldn't have such a paper in his house. He'd fear to have it under his roof and wouldn't touch its filthy pages. Finney's sermon resulted in so many papers thrown out on the street and cancellations, he neither saw nor heard any more opposition from the editors. While at Reading, the great majority of the congregation where Finney preached was converted.

Chapter 14

GOD'S WORD PREVAILS

FROM READING, HE went to Columbia and New York City tearing down religious traditions and doctrinal errors with fabulous results. The fields were ripe for the harvest. After the revival in New York City, he stayed at his father-in-law's home to rest, while deciding where to go next. By this time, Finney had become so well known, he was pressed on every side by churches and ministers to come preach in their area and was at a loss as to which direction to go.

As he began to contemplate the different avenues of opportunity, he inquired into the circumstances at Rochester, NY. There were three Presbyterian churches in Rochester, all with their own problems. The Third Presbyterian Church's pastor had recently left and the church was in a low spiritual condition. The Second Presbyterian Church had considerable division within the church and the pastor was planning on leaving soon. A dispute the First Presbyterian Church had with an elder of the Third Church was about to be tried by the presbytery. Of all the avenues of opportunity, Rochester seemed to be the least inviting of them all.

Finney met with some of his trusted friends to pray and seek wise counsel. They advised him to go east to Philadelphia and New York City, rather than west to Rochester. They were unanimous in the opinion that Rochester had too many problems and stubborn hearts to produce good fruit. Finney was inclined to agree and prepared to head for New York City the next morning. But when he returned home, God began to question him:

> "What are the reasons that deter you from going to Rochester?" I could readily enumerate them; but then the question returned-"Ah! But are these good reasons? Certainly you are needed at Rochester all the more because of these difficulties. Do you shun the field because there are so many things that need to be corrected, because there is so much that is wrong? But if all was right, you would not be needed."[14]

Finney realized he, as well as his friends, had been wrong and was trying to go the most comfortable route. In this generation of America's prosperity, comfort, and entertainment, how many times do we seek the comfortable way instead of God's way? How many times do we attempt to avoid difficult circumstances instead of doing what we know is right? Sometimes, God may send us to the most difficult, weed-infested fields in order to save the wheat. Would we be willing?

Finney felt ashamed that he would shrink from his work for God's kingdom due to difficulties. But in the end, he was willing. He was confident God was with him. Sometimes God will send us into what appears to be difficult circumstances. But He will always give us the grace to overcome and endure. He will always give us His peace to help us accomplish His purposes in the midst of trials.

Revival in an Unlikely Place

Finney conducted the meetings in Rochester in the year 1830. As mentioned, much of the opposition from churches in the eastern United States had begun to subside, until by the time Finney preached at Rochester, he felt no opposition. Shortly after he arrived and began preaching, the atmosphere of the churches at Rochester changed from strife and mistrust to cooperation. It was at the Rochester revival that Finney's meetings of inquiry emerged into what is today known as public altar calls, and he began giving them on a regular basis. During this time, the thought came to him; there must be some type of public action to demonstrate one's commitment to Christ rather than just mental assent. There must be a definite moment, turning point, or decision of faith in one's life to mark his or her conversion; a way to let the world know they're coming out from the ranks of the ungodly to become a disciple of Christ. He made the call in Rochester for them to come forward, as a public demonstration of their commitment to Christ. To his surprise, a much larger number came forward than expected.

Unlike the small frontier towns when Finney first began conducting the revivals, the Rochester revival saw many upper class, professionals, and intellectuals become interested in God. A large number of leading lawyers in the state of New York resided at Rochester, of whom many came to Finney's revival, giving their hearts to God. So Finney's decision to face the difficulties in Rochester yielded high dividends. The majority of leading citizens in Rochester were converted, significantly altering the future of the city.

The revival so affected the spiritual climate of the city, the subsequent years saw a sharp reduction in crime rate, despite the city's steady growth in population. It was reported about one hundred thousand people connected themselves to a church during the revival at Rochester. Dr. Beecher, one of the prominent ministers who had once opposed him, remarked it was the greatest revival the world had ever seen in such a short time. The fame of the Rochester revival spread throughout the land and people came from other states to attend the revival. Had Finney considered the rumors labeling Rochester as a difficult place to preach and followed the inclinations of his own understanding, he may have missed this grand opportunity to change the lives and future of this city.

Motives of the Heart

In his first visit to Providence, R.I., there was a case involving the conversion of a young woman, a Miss Ainsworth, which revealed a subtle truth. This was a young lady of great personal beauty, not only physically, but intellectually, as well. She seemed to listen to every word Finney said with utmost attention. A few days after Finney's sermons, this young lady asked to see him. Her earnest look had drawn Finney's attention, so he remembered exactly who she was.

After briefly conversing with her, he felt she still wasn't convicted enough to realize her sins. Until now, she couldn't see her need for the righteousness of Christ. He began to ask her searching questions regarding her soul. He asked her if she had ever been envious, self-righteous, proud, or vain. She admitted to none of these vices. Although unconverted, she had an excellent reputation among her acquaintances at Providence. Her convictions began to deepen, as Finney conversed with her. With the look of dissatisfaction, she left.

A couple of days later, she asked to see Finney again. This time, she entered the room with a humble, sad countenance. Since her previous conversation with Finney, God had revealed to her how she had acted with insincerity and pretense. She confessed the reason she had refrained from wickedness wasn't because she didn't have evil desires; it wasn't to please God or to obey His commandments, but to protect her reputation. Her fear of men rather than her fear of God kept her from fulfilling evil desires. She had been so flattered and spoiled because of her physical beauty, she had become self-centered and maintained her reputation from purely selfish motives. After receiving further instruction from Finney concerning salvation, she prayed with him and unreservedly gave her life to Christ.

How many of us have deep, dark desires and restrain ourselves from sin, just so we can please men and not get caught? How many times have we appeared on the surface to be righteous so we wouldn't suffer the consequences of punishment from men, rather than out of a pure love for God? How many times have we attempted to protect our reputation rather than our relationship with God?

Sometimes, parents discipline their children's bad behavior out of concern for their reputation rather than love for the child or concern for the child's soul. The results are the child is more concerned with his outward actions; what people think, than for his relationship with God. This type of attitude will result in secret sins. We may attempt to hide these sins from others and never truly repent before God. As long as we continue this façade, our bondage to these secret sins will continue. Openness and honesty with God bring true deliverance.

All of Satan's strategies couldn't hinder God's truth from marching on. His Word does not return void. God's Word continued to prevail in Finney's revivals.

Chapter 15

GROWING INFLUENCE

THE CONTROVERSY OVER slavery first arose in the 1830's when Finney had moved to New York City for a period of time to establish new churches there. Finney, along with other businessmen and church members, began a work in a largely un-churched area of New York City. They purchased a theater to hold services and hundreds were converted. Later, they built a church called the Broadway Tabernacle.

While working in New York City, he occasionally made reference to the indecency of slavery, but wisely decided this wasn't the time to overly emphasize the vices of slavery. Having decided the general public in America wasn't ready to receive the abolitionist message, he continued to make and disciple new converts. For the most part, he avoided the topic of slavery, teaching principals of revival instead. Still, a rumor circulated that the new facility being built would allow whites and blacks to sit together. This caused such a stir in New York City, someone set fire to Broadway Tabernacle, which was under construction at the time, and the firemen refused to put out the flames. Nevertheless, it was rebuilt and eventually finished.

Having traveled and worked almost nonstop for the past ten years, he was beginning to experience fatigue, which resulted in some health problems. He was forced to slow down and spend more time resting. At this time, Finney began to realize there was much more work to be done in the area of revival than he could possibly do as one man. This burden became so heavy, he spent a whole day in fervent, travailing prayer.

In answer to this prayer, a series of Finney's lectures on revival were printed in a periodical, known as *The New York Evangelist,* edited by Rev. Joshua Leavitt. The lectures were afterwards published in a book entitled, *Finney's Lectures on Revivals.* It was circulated throughout Europe and the colonies of Great Britain, as well as the United States. The book impacted nations far beyond what he imagined. Many from all over the world expressed to Finney how this book had impacted their lives. Some who were converted through this book became prominent ministers of the gospel. In addition, he later wrote two volumes of Systematic Theology. Indeed, he relates there were many times God answered his prayers far beyond what he expected.

In 1835, he was asked to help form the Oberlin Collegiate Institute. He agreed to teach theology at the college with the condition blacks would be given the same opportunity to attend as whites and there would be a non-discriminatory policy with regard to race. The trustees of the college agreed, and appointed him as professor of theology. Hence, Oberlin College became the first institution of higher learning in the United States to practice an admissions policy of non-discrimination based on race. Their inclination toward anti-slavery drew hostility from the surrounding towns in the state of Ohio. Many opposed the opening of Oberlin College, while some even threatened to tear down the newly erected buildings. Finney undauntedly stood for what he knew in his heart was right, despite stiff opposition.

Partly because of Oberlin's strong stance against slavery and also due to the economic crash of 1837, the school, and particularly Finney, struggled with finances during the early years of the college. Most men of wealth in New York City who promised Finney support, if he would teach at Oberlin College, were financially humbled during the economic crash, and were unable to fulfill their promises. The faculty faced poverty and trials for a number of years, trusting God for their daily necessities. One winter, Finney was forced to sell some of his personal belongings to replace a cow which had been lost. But in His faithfulness, God moved upon the heart of a friend in Providence, R.I. He sent Finney enough money each year to somewhat offset the lost endowment he had expected from his friends in New York City.

In addition, opposition toward Oberlin College came from ministers and professors of other churches and universities. Partly due to envy and partly to a misunderstanding of Finney's views on perfection and sanctification, ministers far and near actively opposed and misrepresented the theology taught at Oberlin College. Though none publicly admitted it, perhaps it was also due in part to the college's leanings towards anti-slavery.

The faculty at Oberlin responded by turning this persecution over to the Lord. They left the opposition alone, refraining from unfruitful arguments. Instead, they continued tending to their business of running the school and teaching the students. God blessed their efforts. Although they had to make sacrifices, there was never a shortage of funds, which they couldn't overcome. God had a remnant of people who weren't moved by the controversies surrounding Oberlin College, but supported them faithfully. Moreover, the college continued to grow and seemed to have all the students it could handle. As the work continued, God's power was evident. The opposition couldn't deny its results.

Oberlin College under Finney's influence became innovative and famous. Oberlin College was at the cutting edge in understanding and applying truth from the Bible, which led them to fight prejudice in any form. The first four females in the nation to receive a B.A. did so at Oberlin College. As mentioned, it was one of the first colleges to admit black students without regard to race. They also pioneered the way for a desegregated church. Blacks could sit anywhere they chose in the church where the students attended. In addition, it was among the first to allow blacks and whites to sit at the same tables for lunch in the school cafeteria. When the first blacks began attending Oberlin College, some of the white students asked the administration to give the blacks a place to sit alone. When the school officials met to discuss this problem, Finney proposed that these white students making the request be given tables to sit alone, and so it was approved. The black students sat in the cafeteria with everyone else. The white students who objected had the opportunity to sit alone.

Their knowledge of the truth within God's Word led them to teach strict discipline in moral and ethical behavior. Lewd jokes, sexual innuendos, and immorality were strictly forbidden among the students. These practices at first drew much opposition from the surrounding community disguised in different forms. However, parents soon began to realize how safe their daughters were in such an atmosphere. As a result, enrollment in Oberlin College increased every year, especially with women. Finney customarily taught at Oberlin during the spring and summer, while leading revivals in various parts of the nation during the fall and winter.

Spiritual Warfare

After opposition from the Eastern states had waned, Finney held a revival campaign in the Boston area. When Finney arrived in Boston in the fall of 1843, he was met with a strong Unitarian influence. The orthodox ministers tried convincing the Unitarians with debating skills. They tried convincing the Unitarians with their orthodoxy, rather than God's Word administered by the Holy Spirit's power. It was Finney's belief that if these orthodox ministers demonstrated the gospel's power by living what they preached, the Unitarians would believe and be converted.

The Unitarians needed to see evidence in the lives of Christians that Jesus was really able to give them power to overcome sin. But it seemed their profession of faith in Christ didn't agree with their experiences. For the most part, they weren't living out the gospel they were professing. Their teaching amounted to empty words, void of the gospel's power. They were bound by tradition, too formal to allow the freedom of the Holy Spirit. Finney blames the Christians' timidity in Boston for the lack of true revival. The Unitarians had often criticized them. They were afraid of what the press and public might say. Accordingly, they became overly cautious, afraid to address controversial issues such as sin, judgment, and eternal hell. This made it more difficult to counter the influence of Unitarianism and endangered the impenitent souls.

> But my righteous one will live by faith. And if he shrinks back, I will not be pleased with him.
>
> —Hebrews 10:38

When Finney first began preaching in Boston, many were unaccustomed to his confrontational style of preaching. He preached, not only to the unbelievers, but to Christians as well. At the time in Boston, most sermons were non-confrontational; those messages designed, not to convict an audience, but to edify and make them feel good about themselves. But these types of sermons also set a low standard of godliness and did much harm to the Christians in Boston. Much to his surprise, Finney's soul searching sermons caused many Church members in Boston to shrink back from attending the meetings. Finney remarked he had never seen professing Christians shrink back from his convicting sermons as they did in Boston.

At first many Church members were astonished and even offended by his uncompromising style of preaching. They weren't accustomed to such plain spoken rebuke and correction; such fearless preaching. But as the work continued, their attitude changed and they came to greatly appreciate Finney's soul searching sermons.

As was common at this time, many clergy in Boston held the belief that becoming a Christian and living an overcoming Christian life was all up to the Holy Spirit; a person had nothing to do with his regeneration. Finney asserted this as only a half truth. The Holy Spirit can influence and make His power available to help bring about repentance in our lives, but the person also has a part to play in the regeneration of his soul. Finney taught how our will and choices play a major role in making a lasting change in our lives. Not only does it depend on the Holy Spirit's power, but on our attitude and willingness to repent.

After a time of preaching the truth in Boston, God's word with the Holy Spirit's anointing had time to take root and grow in the churches. The revival began to have good results as a large number of people were converted to Christ throughout the city. Indeed, God's Word doesn't return void (Isaiah 55:10-11).

In the fall and winter of 1843, when Finney was preaching the revival campaign in Boston, he endured intense spiritual warfare. This spiritual warfare tried his beliefs. It seemed as if a dark cloud prevented him from remembering the wonderful experiences, fellowship, and revelation with God he had previously known. It was difficult to lay hold of the former communion and divine assurance he had once experienced. He felt darkness surround him and had momentary doubts of his ministry and even his own salvation. What if his beliefs only stemmed from his emotions rather than the truth? He spent much time in agonizing prayer. He awoke every day at 4:00 A.M. and prayed until 8:00 A.M. before he started the day's activities.

In the midst of this darkness Finney entrusted himself unto God as a small child does his loving parents. No matter what happened, he determined to totally surrender himself to God, knowing God would take care of him as a loving mother does her child. He gave up his struggle to remember the former blessings and resolved to rest in God, no matter what the future held.

Finney emerged from this spiritual battle stronger than before. He ascended to new realms of faith and assurance. He obtained an even higher knowledge of God's grace than before. He received a fresh anointing of the Holy Spirit. His state of mind entered into perfect peace and rest. Christ had renewed his first love and lifted him into a higher spiritual realm than he had ever known before. The Bible seemed ablaze with fresh revelation of his relationship to Christ; what Christ had done for him. His anxieties, cares, and concerns seemed to vanish. He experienced a new refreshing of joy. From this time forward he abided with Christ as never before.

This newfound joy was briefly interrupted a few years later with the death of his wife. But as the Holy Spirit revealed to him the joy she was experiencing in heaven with Christ, Finney was able to resume the blessed state of rest which he had learned to enjoy by trusting in God. Instead of sorrow he rejoiced with his departed wife.

I'm convinced spiritual warfare often precedes great breakthroughs and opportunities. It was shortly after this intense spiritual warfare and great personal loss that some of Finney's greatest opportunities came.

In 1848 he married Elizabeth Ford Atkinson and his second wife traveled with him teaching at women's prayer meetings and ministering one on one to women.

Bearing Fruit in England

In 1849, he traveled to England and stayed for about a year preaching revival campaigns. He came at the invitation of Mr. Potto Brown.

Mr. Brown, a very benevolent man who had great concern for the poor, was in the milling business. He had a vision to build schools and educate the poor, whom had been greatly neglected. Mr. Brown saw how the churches in England had failed in effectively reaching out to the poor. At Mr. Brown's invitation Finney began in England by preaching to the poor and lower class. Having already begun the work of educating the masses of the lower class and building a chapel, Mr. Brown threw his heart and soul into the work of revival, assisting Finney with whatever was needed. The gospel spread and was gladly received among these villages of the poor. Before Finney left, every one of Mr. Brown's friends, whom he had been working with to build schools, had been converted to Christ. The revival among the poor in this region continued for years, even after Finney had returned to the United States.

When news spread of Finney's arrival in England, he received multitudes of invitations. He felt pressed by the Spirit to accept invitations to preach in other cities of England. To Finney it seemed the majority of these invitations were for the purpose of raising funds for various projects such as building chapels, schools, or to help pay for the pastor's salary. Finney recalls that had he complied with such invitations, he'd have had time for nothing else. So he decided to decline all such invitations. Finney informed them he didn't come to England to raise money for himself or anyone else, but for the sole purpose of winning souls. As was typical of Finney's revival meetings, his preaching was accompanied by deep conviction, weeping, and in some cases anguish over the condition of the soul.

Some clergy in America who long opposed Finney's revivals, communicated with influential church leaders of England, portraying him as a heretical fanatic. For this reason these ministers of England were hesitant to support Finney's campaigns. Being men of noble character, they didn't publicly oppose or support him, but searched the matter to find if the accusations were true. Once Finney began ministering and they saw how God blessed his preaching, they began to question Finney's accusers.

Several well respected church leaders in England talked to Finney about his doctrines and obtained his books on systematic theology. Upon examining his work, they found nothing which warranted such accusations against him. Once they threw their support behind him, revival spread throughout England in a powerful manner and Finney met with much success during his tenure there.

Finney labored tirelessly in the harvest fields of England, sacrificing his time and energy. He even declined to go on sightseeing tours so he could use every moment to win souls. Finney received so many invitations wherever he went in England; he couldn't possibly accept all of them. Seeing the hunger and great need among the people, Finney began to recommend his wife, Elizabeth, to speak at some of the invitations.

Unaccustomed to speaking at public meetings, she was at first hesitate to accept these invitations. In this generation, women did very little in public speaking. She began by only conducting women's meetings. Most men at this time were prejudice against women speaking in public meetings. However, God was with Elizabeth and her meetings produced very good results. The men also began attending her meetings. So his wife as well, worked hard to win souls. Finney and his wife were speaking at separate meetings as they traveled throughout England.

Eventually, Finney went to London. The spiritual climate in London was so cold and indifferent, Finney felt the need to remain there for extensive work. Finney describes how the Spirit of Prayer came upon him for the people of London. At times the Spirit moved upon him in such a powerful way he could hardly stop praying. Finney describes it as being almost out of himself in the Spirit of prayer.

He preached at Whitefield's Tabernacle, for nine months, resulting in thousands being converted. Dr. John Campbell was pastor of Whitefield's Tabernacle. The Tabernacle held up to 3,000 seats, but Finney suggests there was such interest in the revival, up to 40,000 people would have attended had they found a facility with such seating capacity.

The spiritual climate in London had been in such a weak state, very few weekly sermons were preached. Dr. Campbell once commented that Finney probably preached to more people in the week evenings than all the rest of the ministers in London together. During this time, Finney was able to preach to a group of scholars. Finney explained how their education could be a blessing if they used it rightly or curse if they used it selfishly. This lecture resulted in the conversion of many scholars.

Eventually England's damp climate and unceasing labor took a toll on both Finney and his wife so they became very hoarse. Upon visiting with Finney, his good friend, Potto Brown, became concerned when he saw their state of health. Mr. Brown knew Finney and his wife would never be able to rest in England. By this time they had become rather famous in London. They couldn't go far without being recognized. Besides, Finney had such a passion for souls, he could hardly keep himself from preaching to them. With godly wisdom and concern Brown insisted they to go to France for a nice long vacation to rest and recuperate. Finney wasn't as well known among the French. Mr. Brown perceived Finney had a better chance to rest in France. Since he didn't speak their language, Finney wouldn't be as inclined to continue laboring for souls as long as he was in France. He gave them 50 pounds and sent them to Paris. They also visited other parts of France avoiding the public. They remained in France for six weeks during the winter season. The long vacation worked. They were able to fully recover their health. After six weeks in France, they were able to return to their labors in London.

Finally, after a year working in the harvest fields of England, Finney and Elizabeth made preparations for their return voyage to America. With reluctance, Finney and his wife left for home after a very successful tour in England. On the day they set sail, a crowd of people gathered to see them off, mostly new converts. With tears in their eyes and love in their hearts, the ship set sail; their labors in England ended.

Chapter 16

THE LATTER YEARS

UPON RETURNING TO the United States, Finney resumed his custom of teaching at Oberlin during the spring and summer, and conducting revival campaigns across the land during the fall and winter. His revivals continued to have success, and at the same time drew opposition from various clergymen.

At one point, Finney stated some ministers personally expressed their support to him, but opposed him with their actions or never came out publicly in support of his ministry. He indicates he never really understood this seemingly hypocrisy from some of the clergymen. It is thought some of the clergy opposed him because he wasn't educated in their theological schools. Others perhaps supported him in their hearts, but feared losing their status or reputations among those who opposed him. There were those well meaning ministers who were convinced Finney's revivals spawned too much fanaticism. While some outbursts may have been fanaticism, most were demonstrations of the Holy Spirit resulting in changed lives. Some in the Eastern United States, having been influenced by Unitarianism, thought his sermons too harsh and negative.

Nevertheless, God was with Finney. His preaching was successful among the laypersons and ordinary people, which demonstrated if God is in the work, no man, can stop it. There were many ministers who esteemed Finney and labored alongside him to bring in a harvest of souls.

By the time Finney revisited areas in the state of New York, where he began his ministry almost thirty years earlier, most opposition in the area had subsided. The revivals were so pure, the Holy Spirit's conviction so apparent, many involved with the earlier opposition in upstate New York confessed their mistake and urged him to return to the areas once again. The revivals weren't just emotional fanaticism, but produced results which lasted. Many years later, the revivals were still bearing good fruit. Consequently, in the latter years of Finney's ministry, there was less open opposition. His sincerity, character, and labors had earned him respect from all denominations. Forty years later Finney drew much favor and support rather than the opposition he experienced in the early years. Still, there was always some type of resistance to Finney's revivals, though less in his later years. The opposition was usually from clergymen. By Finney's latter years much of the church had concluded the methods pursued by the opposition to discredit Finney's revivals were unwise, unjust, and unchristian.

In the early 1850's, Finney revisited the towns of Rome, and Rochester with good results. He conducted a total of three campaigns in Rochester during his lifetime. He asserted in his memoirs how he had never preached with more pleasure anywhere than in Rochester. In each revival at Rochester, it began with the professionals, the upper class, and trickled down to the lower class. Finney credits the revivals at Rochester as having a higher degree of success than most any other area where he preached. He attributes this success to the people's willingness to receive the truth.

He speaks of New England having a formality and stiffness which stifled the moving of the Holy Spirit. They had a set way of doing things, afraid to allow the Holy Spirit any freedom to move in new and different ways. One of Finney's acquaintances, a fellow minister, described it as putting the Holy Spirit into a straight jacket. The Holy Spirit was hindered in His work at New England by pride, self-wisdom, and prejudice. Finney believed this was in part due to the opposition at one time of several influential ministers, the same ones who attempted to stir up opposition in England.

But in Rochester, there was love, good-will, and liberty which allowed God's Spirit to move unhindered, without the danger of extravagance, fanaticism, or disorder. As with any movement of God, there's always some who go beyond the Holy Spirit's leading into excess and fanaticism. To be sure, most of these accusations, according to Finney, were simply wrong ideas of what constituted disorder. Most churches viewed anything they weren't accustomed to as disorder. Their stereotyped ways limited the infinite God of the universe. Finney's third revival in Rochester produced a great harvest just as the two previous ones.

In the fall of 1856 through the winter of 1858, he preached at Boston for two consecutive fall/winter seasons. Once again, some influential ministers were uncooperative in their support of the revival, some even opposing it.

He mentions a great revival prevailing in the northern states at this time. He gives interesting insight concerning this revival. It was led in large part by the church's laity, rather than the ministers. The people preferred going to prayer meetings over attending lectures or sermons. According to Finney this revival almost left the ministers in the shade. They didn't openly oppose it. At the same time they weren't an influential part of it.

It began with daily prayer meetings all across the northern states. It was as if God was pumping the northern states with a huge breath of life before the War Between the States began. Finney referred to the War Between the States as the great rebellion. It was estimated over fifty thousand conversions occurred per week in the northern states during this period of time. No doubt, many of these converts would later fight in the War Between the States, some never returning, having died on the battlefield. This great revival enabled many of the Civil War casualties to enter into the glorious rest of heaven's bliss, as opposed to eternal damnation, had not this revival taken place.

Why were many ministers for the most part left out of this great revival? God knew unless there was a drastic change in the people's hearts, judgment was on the way. He knew the dark times which lay ahead for the United States. It wasn't a time for eloquent sermons or lectures, but a time of intercession for men's souls and the destiny of a nation. God knew that the only way to avoid the coming disaster could be found in intercessory prayer.

Could it be God's original intention was for the clergy to lead in prayer; to conduct more prayer meetings rather than preaching and teaching? Is it possible the clergy were so set in the content of their meetings, they didn't hear the Holy Spirit beckoning them to a season of prayer? Perhaps this is why He moved upon the laity to form prayer meetings outside the church's regular meetings. It was the ministers' choice whether or not they decided to participate. Most of them, busy with pastoral duties, chose not to participate, so the laity became the leaders of these prayer meetings.

Therefore, God used the lay influence rather than clergy to bring about His next movement within the church. This revival was carried on by prayer meetings, personal visitation, conversations, and distribution of tracts by the laity. Having received instruction on God's Word, the laity felt it time for them to begin the work through prayer and evangelism.

Finney implies that although the northern states were experiencing great revival, the southern states seemed to be preoccupied with preserving their institution of slavery. Instead of turning their thoughts toward God, they focused on the problem of preserving their way of life on the plantation. According to Finney they were in such an angry, irritated state over the question of slavery, they grieved away the Holy Spirit. I'm convinced, had the southern states participated in daily prayer as their brothers to the north, the War Between the States could have been averted.

Return to England

Meanwhile, the revival was so sweeping in the northern states with ministers and laity taking part, Finney felt he was more needed in England. By now Finney's reputation was so renowned, everywhere he went the people expected a great revival. He was highly respected much as Billy Graham is in his generation. Faith and expectation play a key role in revival. Like Enoch, Noah, Elijah, and John the Baptist, Finney walked with God. Everywhere Finney went, God's presence was manifested in a marvelous way.

He labored in England until 1860. Everywhere Finney went in England people repented and souls were saved. At one point Finney's health began to falter and he thought he may return home to Oberlin. He went back to Potto Brown's place in Houghton, England to rest for a season. After a few weeks at Potto Brown's house with only marginal improvement, Dr. Foster invited Finney to stay at his house to see if he could help him. Dr. Foster had eight children whom were unconverted. He was particularly troubled about his eldest son who also was a physician of remarkable talents. He was very affectionate toward his father, yet he was skeptical about the things of God. This unbelief deeply hurt his father.

Finney waited for an opportunity to talk to the young physician about his skepticism. He drew the young man out for a walk and conversed with him about his beliefs. With the help of God, Finney succeeded in revealing the fallacy of the young doctor's views. The foundations of the young man's philosophy collapsed and he became confounded in the presence of truth. Consequently, he became very anxious about his soul. After another three weeks at Dr. Foster's, Finney's health improved enough that he was once again able to preach.

A few days later Finney preached one Sabbath evening on the text, "The hail shall sweep away the refuges of lies, and the waters shall overflow the hiding places. Your covenant with death shall be disannulled and your agreement with hell shall not stand."[15] That night Dr. Foster's son couldn't sleep he was so anxious for his soul. He committed his life to Christ passing from death into life. During the revival, every one of Dr. Foster's children was converted. This family's house became a joyful place with love abounding. The revival spread from the church to the professors of theology and extensively among the unconverted throughout the town.

Having regained his health, Finney continued preaching in Scotland and England with great results. Upon departing Liverpool on his return trip to the States, many people of England assembled to bid him farewell, just as believers did for the apostle Paul on his missionary journeys (Acts 20:36-38). Undoubtedly, Finney received considerable satisfaction from his labors in England.

There's no mention of his wife, Elizabeth, accompanying him on his second trip to England. It's probable she was struggling with failing health, preventing her from traveling to England. In 1863, about three years after his return from England, he lost his second wife. Finney says little in his memoirs about the death of his first wife, Lydia, and even less about the death of Elizabeth. He concentrated his memoirs on the Holy Spirit's work in the revivals rather than his personal life. He only mentions his family as it related to the ministry.

In the final chapter of his memoirs, Finney returns home to Oberlin. Those in Oberlin had greatly pressured him to return home, implying the church and Bible College were in trouble. Otherwise Finney admits he would've remained in England for another year or two. Even though exhausted from his long voyage from England, Finney began his labor in Oberlin immediately. New students had just begun attending the college and many new people had moved into the town as it continued to grow. As a result, Finney asserts there were many unrepentant and unconverted students and persons when he returned to Oberlin. He began daily prayer meetings and spoke in the churches. Revival began to sweep the town of Oberlin.

The pressure of his labors increased from week to week. He labored intensely for four months until he was overcome with chills and exhaustion. He was confined to his bed for over two months. Hence, the revival in Oberlin gradually waned until the summer when he was able to resume his preaching. From 1860 to 1867 this pattern in Oberlin continued. In the fall when the new students arrived, Finney overworked until he was overcome with fatigue and confined to his house and bed for three months.

In 1865 he married Rebecca Allen Rayl. She also helped Finney in the ministry. Although many churches all over the nation and the world urged him to come and preach at their churches, Finney declined due to his lack of stamina. In his 70's now, he preferred the home comforts and nursing at the Bible college in Oberlin. Anyone who desired to hear him preach had to travel to Oberlin. He eventually discontinued preaching in the evenings because the excitement prevented him from sleeping during the night.

Finney's writings emphasized personal holiness and rejected Calvinism. In Finney's opinion, one who professed to be a Christian while continuing to practice unrepentant sin, must immediately repent or be lost.

Finney's memoirs end in December of 1868. In 1875, Charles Grandison Finney left this earth to enter into eternal rest, but his work still lives on. His book of memoirs contains many pages and is very extensive. Even so, Finney asserts he was only able to record a few of the interesting and striking occurrences as he remembered. I believe the Holy Spirit brought into his remembrance important aspects of the revivals which blessed and will continue to benefit future generations; truth which lays a solid foundation of doctrine and methods for revival. I'm sure Finney could have written volumes of memoirs.

The apostle John concluded his gospel by saying there wasn't a book large enough to contain all the teaching, miracles, and kind acts of Jesus (John 21:25). Similarly, the same can be said about Finney's revivals. His lifetime of hard work reaped a bountiful harvest of souls. He lived a rich, rewarding life, redeeming his time here on the earth. He undoubtedly recorded his memoirs with a deep satisfaction and contentment. He could say as the apostle Paul, "I have fought the good fight, I have finished the race, and I have kept the faith. There is now in store for me a crown of righteousness" (2 Timothy 4:7-8).

Finney was a great revivalist, a preacher of righteousness. Some may conclude, with convincing evidence, he was the Billy Graham of the nineteenth century. His life and books continue to impact thousands in subsequent generations. Indeed, as the old *Battle Hymn of the Republic* decrees, "His Truth is marching on."

Chapter 17

WHAT IS A PREACHER OF RIGHTEOUSNESS?

WHAT SET THESE men apart from the rest of their generation? Firstly, these preachers of righteousness had a deep desire to know God and to fellowship with Him. This burning desire to know their creator enabled them to know His voice. They learned to listen and to know their Shepherd's voice (John 10:3). They spent years listening to the Master's voice, learning His ways. Consequently, when the time came for their public ministry, they had something to say because they had been with the Righteous One.

Secondly, they were ordinary men from ordinary backgrounds who had faith in an extraordinary God. He called men and women from all walks of life, from the well educated Pharisees such as Nicodemus and Paul, to the poor and illiterate. Most of his followers weren't the wealthy, educated, and elite. They weren't leaders of the established religions or the sons of well known leaders.

Elisha was plowing with twelve yoke of oxen when God instructed Elijah to single him out. Saul, who became the first king of Israel, was also a farmer. David was a shepherd boy. Others whom God called were farmers, fishermen, shepherds, tax collectors, even harlots such as Rahab. When God calls a man or woman he doesn't look at their education, wealth, or pedigree. He doesn't even look at their natural talents. God looks upon the heart. It wasn't their talents, charm, or good looks which made these men and women special, but God's anointing. It wasn't their wealth or education, but their willingness and faith to obey.

These men preached of God's justice to their generation, warning of judgments to come. They also declared the way of escape through repentance and God's mercy. As we near the Lord's coming, God will raise up preachers of righteousness like Noah, Enoch, Elijah, John the Baptist, and Charles Finney. As the Lord's return nears, even now in our generation, there are preachers of righteousness whom God is preparing. God is communing with them and sharing His thoughts. They are learning to hear the Lord's voice. Like John the Baptist for much of his life, some are still publicly unknown. But God knows them and will raise them up in their season to prepare the way of the Lord. They will be called great in the Lord's sight. They will preach in the spirit of Elijah and none of their words will fall to the ground. They will preach repentance, justice, and salvation through Jesus Christ, the Ark of mercy. They will confront deception with truth. These preachers of righteousness won't be afraid to confront ruthless leaders who have the power to put them to death. They will teach of justice and mercy. Many, some even in the Church, will attempt to discredit these preachers. They may be called negative, mean spirited, and even cruel because of their boldness in proclaiming the truth. However, God will be their witness, even as He was with Elijah. The Word will be preached in power and demonstration; signs and wonders following. Mercy and compassion will come to those who repent, but justice and judgment to those who reject the truth. Through faith in Jesus Christ, we can receive the promise of righteousness. Although those who stand for truth may suffer persecution in this life, they will be spared from the judgments to come. We look for rewards in a better place to come (Hebrews 11:10; 15-16); a city whose builder and maker is God (Hebrews 13:12-14); the New Jerusalem coming down out of heaven where God, Himself will live with man (Hebrews 12:22; Rev 3:12; 21:2).

And what more shall I say? I do not have time to tell about Gideon, Barak, Samson, Jephthah, David, Samuel and the prophets, who through faith conquered kingdoms, administered justice, and gained what was promised; who shut the mouths of lions, quenched the fury of the flames, and escaped the edge of the sword; whose weakness was turned to strength; and who became powerful in battle and routed foreign armies. Women received back their dead, raised to life again. Others were tortured and refused to be released, so that they might gain a better resurrection. Some faced jeers and flogging, while still others were chained and put in prison. They were stoned they were sawed in two; they were put to death by the sword. They went about in sheepskins and goatskins, destitute, persecuted and mistreated— the world was not worthy of them. They wandered in deserts and mountains, and in caves and holes in the ground. These were all commended for their faith, yet none of them received what had been promised. God had planned something better for us so that only together with us would they be made perfect.

—Hebrews 11:32-38

ENDNOTES

1. Alfred Rahlfs et al., "The Wisdom of Solomon", *Good News Bible with Deuterocanonicals/Apocrypha: Today's English Version* (New York: American Bible Society, 1992), p. 356.
2. C. Austin Miles, "In the Garden," *The Broadman Hymnal,* ed. B. B. McKinney (Nashville: Broadman Press, 1940), p. 356.
3. Garth M. Rosell and Richard A. G. Dupuis, *The Original Memoirs of Charles G. Finney,* (Grand Rapids, Michigan: Zondervan, 2002), p. 9.
4. Ibid., p. 11.
5. Ibid., p. 16.
6. Ibid., p. 2.
7. Ibid., p. 327.
8. Ibid., p. 190.
9. Ibid., p. 137.
10. Ibid., p. 80.
11. Ibid., pp. 53-54.
12. Ibid., pp. 134-135.
13. Ibid., pp. 157-158.
14. Ibid., p. 139.
15. Ibid., p. 418.

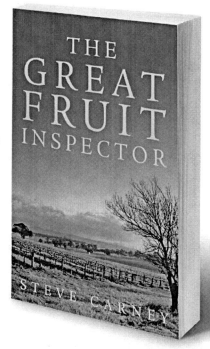

CPSIA information can be obtained at www.ICGtesting.com
Printed in the USA
LVOW080157310113

317916LV00002B/11/P